# the
# Mata
# Hari

# Mountain Biker's
## Road
## Trip

Other titles in this series

**the Mad Keen Golfer's Road Trip**

**the Mad Keen Fisherman's Road Trip**

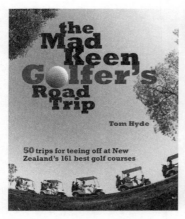 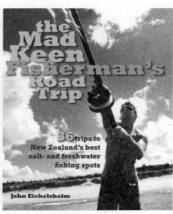

and coming in 2008

**the Mad Keen Wine Buff's Road Trip**

# the Mad Keen Mountain Biker's Road Trip

**Ruth Connor**

RANDOM HOUSE
NEW ZEALAND

Disclaimer: All tracks in this book were ridden for research (and fun) purposes in the 12 months before publication and all information within was correct as far as we knew at the time of publication. However, things can change quickly in the outdoors; tracks can deteriorate, markers can fall over, bridges can be washed away, land and track access can change. Check with local DOC (Department of Conservation) offices or information centres for current information. The author accepts no responsibility or liability for injury or loss associated with any activity detailed in this book.

A catalogue record for this book is available from the National Library of New Zealand

A RANDOM HOUSE BOOK
published by
Random House New Zealand
18 Poland Road, Glenfield, Auckland, New Zealand
www.randomhouse.co.nz

Random House International
Random House
20 Vauxhall Bridge Road
London, SW1V 2SA
United Kingdom

Random House Australia (Pty) Ltd
20 Alfred Street, Milsons Point, Sydney,
New South Wales 2061, Australia

Random House South Africa Pty Ltd
Isle of Houghton
Corner Boundary Road and Carse O'Gowrie
Houghton 2198, South Africa

Random House Publishers India Private Ltd
301 World Trade Tower, Hotel Intercontinental Grand Complex,
Barakhamba Lane, New Delhi 110 001, India

First published 2007

© 2007 Ruth Connor
The moral rights of the author have been asserted

ISBN 978 1 86941 884 7

This book is copyright. Except for the purposes of fair reviewing no part of this publication may be reproduced or transmitted in any form or by any means, electronic or mechanical, including photocopying, recording or any information storage and retrieval system, without permission in writing from the publisher.

Maps, graphs and icons: Deborah Hinde
Cover and text design: Nick Turzynski, redinc., Auckland
Layout: Anna Seabrook
Cover photograph: graememurray.com
Printed in China by Everbest Printing Co Ltd

# Contents

# Contents

# Acknowledgements

There are many people who have made contributions to this book, and to whom I am very grateful for their time and enthusiasm. Additionally, there have been many inspirational mountain bikers in my own group of riding friends and acquaintances over the years, and without them I would never have had so much fun and adventure.

So, in no particular order, thanks to Pete Masters, Karl Young, Garry Sullivan, Graeme Murray, Jason Barclay, Hugh Calder, Adam Lovell, Margaret McKenzie, Nicole Newnham, Glenda Keegan, Chris Cowan, Chris from Te Aroha, Chris from Bike & Pack, Trish Wrigley, Tama Easton, Ian Goldschmidt, Phil and Chris Oliver, Bike Parks, John at Bushaven, Lisa at DOC Opotiki, Martin Langley, Alistair Worrall, Carl Larsen, Rachel Chamberlain, Jono Calder, Simon Pearson and especially Paul Blundell.

# Introduction

**This book is for keen mountain bikers who want to make the most of their weekends and trips away. The detailed information about the rides should give you an idea of what you are letting yourself in for without spoiling the surprise. The instructions should ensure that you can find the trail and follow it with minimum fuss, faffing around and, dare I say it, chance of getting lost. It is also for those who want to try something new, to challenge themselves, think outside their local mountain-bike park and get out into the beautiful New Zealand countryside.**

This book is also for people who, despite a love of great mountain biking, realise there are other worthwhile things in life; the opportunity to combine some of these into riding trips may lead to even greater bliss. For people who want to be directed swiftly to an excellent coffee, a good breakfast or a fine meal — or warned that they can't get any of these things — the benefit of insider knowledge is paramount. I've included other tips on accommodation (including camping) and other activities only as seen fit; they're gems I have come across that you probably won't find in the standard tourist guff.

The reality is that most of our mountain-biking trips out of town are confined to weekends, long weekends and a few holidays. So every time you head away with a single track in mind you want to hit the nail on the head. You need to be assured that you are going somewhere with great riding where you won't get lost, bogged down, bush bashed, shut out or misled. Weekends are precious and should be spent riding the best trails possible and enjoying the best of the rest an area has to offer.

The rides in this book have been chosen because they are reliably good or great or sensational. You won't be disappointed by any of them. They are all predominantly single-track rides aimed at the keen mountain biker who likes some technical challenges, has a bit of a sense of adventure and in some cases a sense of humour too. Most of the trails are in native bush, many are through amazing scenery and some feature fascinating historical and geographical points of interest. The rides are grouped so you can work them into a weekend or long weekend without spending too much time in the car between rides.

This book is not trying to be a comprehensive guide to riding in New Zealand, but it is a comprehensive guide to the best (legal) single tracks around the country. There will always be the odd ride that misses the cut because it is too remote, too tricky to find, too overgrown or way too technical. Sadly, many have been left out because of access issues and contention over management of mountain bikers. I like to think of these as future opportunities.

## Skills and fitness

It is a very tricky thing to provide comprehensive and objective gradings for mountain-bike rides or required skill levels for riders. In this book I have decided to use a basic 'minimum required skill level' as an overall guide while taking a more descriptive approach to details of each ride. That way you can decide for yourself if it's suitable for your ability.

The categories used to define the minimum skill level required for each ride relate to your technical ability. They are **recreational**, **intermediate** and **advanced**. Think of them as a continuum. Recreational-level riders are those with some off-road trail experience who are keen to develop their skills and enjoy single-track riding. Intermediate riders are experienced mountain bikers with moderate technical skills who enjoy being challenged by rocky and rooty obstacles, don't mind undulating terrain and like narrower single track that is generally benched. Advanced riders are those who like to be challenged by steep rock and root obstacles, don't mind off-camber trails with some drops and are confident with narrow and exposed tracks. They may expect to do some carrying or pushing on trails due to the more rugged nature. **Please note that there are no rides geared at absolute beginners or those with no riding experience**, except in odd cases where 'family' rides are mentioned.

Fitness and endurance can be a great leveller. A technical genius on the downhills may not have the fitness and stamina to ride all day or attack a four-hour uphill. I have pointed out the rides that you probably won't enjoy — or even finish — if you don't have a good level of fitness and endurance.

The time frames suggested for completing most of these rides are based on how long they would take the average rider within the appropriate skill category.

## Outdoor skills

I've used the term 'outdoor skills' to describe specific knowledge and abilities that may be required in the New Zealand back country. Many of these rides are in remote areas that have no mobile phone coverage or easy road access and are exposed to natural forces and the elements. By outdoor skills, I mean:

*Interpreting weather forecasts* — this means checking the forecast when planning a trip and as near as possible to your departure. Take into account the elevation that you may get to and the exposure of the area. And remember, weather forecasts are not always right!

*Following a track with variable marking* — all the tracks in this book are marked but the type of markers and the distance between them varies between tracks and even within tracks. It is important that you are always sure that you are on the appropriate track and that as soon as you have doubts you return to the most recent sure-point.

*Map-reading skills* — most trips in this book do not require serious map-reading ability. However, for a number of rides, an appropriate topographical map is useful for letting you know where you are and providing backup should things become confusing. Knowing how to use a topographical map — understanding contour lines and being able to orientate yourself with a compass — is an important skill for anyone heading into the back country.

*River-crossing knowledge* — if you don't know how to properly cross a river you shouldn't attempt it. There are only a couple of rides in this book that require these skills, and usually only after reasonable recent rainfall, but heed the warnings because the consequences can be very serious.

*Basic first aid* — if things go wrong in the back country, you need to know what to do and be prepared. The best advice is: don't go into the back country alone; do a first-aid course beforehand; and take a first-aid kit with you. The most useful things in a first-aid kit are usually a roll of strapping tape, wound dressings, bandages, a survival blanket and a box of matches.

*On-the-go bike maintenance* — when you are in the middle of nowhere and things go wrong with your trusty steed you need to have some know-how and/or a MacGyver instinct. At the bare minimum you (or someone in your group) need to know how to change and fix a puncture and repair a broken chain. It's also useful if you can straighten or replace a derailleur hanger, straighten a wheel, and bypass the derailleur to single-speed a bike.

*Tolerance of tricky track conditions* — some of the back-country tracks in this book can suffer from a lack of maintenance. Even if they are maintained regularly a storm or rain can work mischief — you might find yourself having to climb over or circumnavigate large fallen trees, which can be a lot trickier than it might seem when carrying a bike. Slips are another common occurrence that can make tracks unsafe or impassable. It is helpful to report these problems to the local DOC or council office.

## Safety and equipment

Safety first! Wear a helmet and gloves, and glasses for eye protection. Ensure your bike is in good working order. Tell someone where you are going and when you expect to be back. Know the opt-out points, if there are any, should anything go wrong. Lock your car and don't leave valuables visible.

Most keen mountain bikers have a pretty good idea what they need in their backpacks. Here's what I would recommend:

- Water — plenty of it and the ability to purify more.
- Food — both tasty snacks (including emergency jelly babies) and some 'real food' for longer rides.
- Equipment — a pump, tyre levers, at least two spare tubes, a repair kit and a bike tool with chain-breaker.
- Warm clothes, including an extra layer of arms and legs, and an additional top and a jacket.
- Emergency provisions — a mobile phone, money, a basic first-aid kit and a torch.

You're asking for disaster if you head away for a great weekend of mountain biking with a potentially problematic bike. Get it properly serviced and be awake to how things feel and sound. Don't ignore that rattle until something breaks — get it fixed. Even if you don't like to clean your bike regularly, keep the drive-train free of mud and dirt and well oiled. It sounds and feels a whole lot nicer and will prevent chain-suck. Check your tyre pressure with a firm thumb, and check your brakes and gears before you leave home.

## Travel

If you are heading a little further afield on your weekend away, car travel may not be the best option. If you are travelling by air there are a few things worth knowing. Air New Zealand doesn't charge for bikes unless the total luggage weight is outside the allowed 20 kg. You can take your bike on as is, with the handlebars turned around and the drive-train covered. This way the bike is harder to throw from a height, unlike a bike box! Qantas charges separately for bikes and won't take them unless they are in a box.

## Access and advocacy

All the rides in this book are DOC-sanctioned, on private land that's opened up to mountain bikers, or through legal 'paper' roads. The intention here is not to step on anyone's toes. However, there are a number of rides that could not be included because of access issues, something that's quite frustrating.

Until recently, by law, you could not ride your bicycle off-road in a national park. In general this still stands true, but an amendment to the National Parks Act allows for parks to allow bikes on certain tracks. It is hoped that this will pave the way for tracks such as the Heaphy to open to bikes at certain times of the year, in a similar fashion to the Queen Charlotte. This is good progress.

A large potential bike-riding resource is DOC-managed land in forest parks and reserves. A number of forest parks already provide for and encourage mountain bikes. Craigieburn in Canterbury, Mt Richmond near Nelson and Pureora near Taupo are great examples of conservancies proactively catering to mountain bikers and listening to this significant user group. The Kaimanawa Forest Park in the central North Island and the Kaimai Mamaku Forest Park in the Bay of Plenty are examples of the opposite.

Things can be complicated because DOC's access policies vary greatly between conservancies, decisions can seem arbitrary and the decision-making processes are not always transparent or open for public debate. Thus, mountain bikers are shut out of some amazing places, sometimes for no good apparent reason.

The most constructive thing you can do to improve access to these areas is have a say. Make submissions on the conservation management strategies that concern you or talk to the local DOC area manager or conservancy manager. Getting a group of people to make submissions to the conservancies involved can be particularly useful.

Access to land in private ownership can understandably be tricky and often relies on the goodwill of landowners (often forestry companies and farmers). In many cases, access to land may be an informal arrangement and it can be hard to find information about it.

---

### Mountain Bike New Zealand's mountain bikers' code
- Ride mountain-bike and multi-use tracks only. Ask permission (if required) from landowners before heading out.
- Respect other users; always give way to walkers.
- Leave no trace; never skid or drop rubbish.
- Keep your bicycle under control.
- Never spook animals; leave gates as you find them.

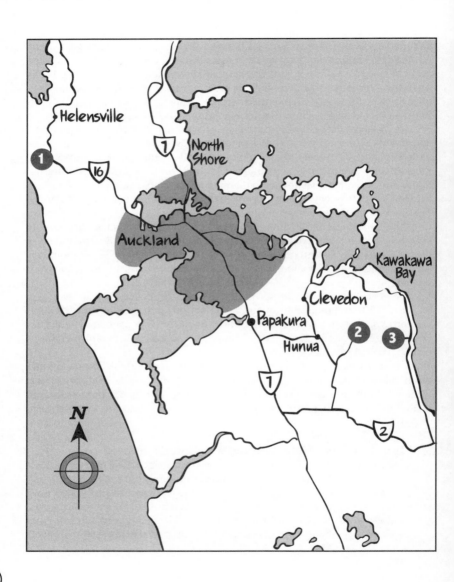

# Auckland

Auckland may seem an unlikely choice for a weekend or long weekend of mountain biking. After all, more than a quarter of our population already lives there and probably wants to head away from the big smoke for a holiday weekend. Those from outside Auckland may not necessarily consider it a major outdoor recreation destination. However, the Auckland region has some great mountain biking, an extensive and varied coastline and an amazing collection of regional parks that provide some pristine camping and recreational opportunities. If you live in Auckland, consider getting away for a weekend not far from home.

My choice of rides in the Auckland area does not cover all the available tracks but it's a highly recommended and varied selection. It covers Auckland's major riding destination, Woodhill Mountain Bike Park to the north-west, which has trails for all abilities and enough to keep you occupied for at least a weekend. The lovely and worthwhile Moumoukai Farm Track in the Hunua Ranges Regional Park south-east of the city is the pick of the south's purpose-built tracks and is suitable for all levels of riders. The last ride is not well known but it's a fun ride in Waharau Regional Park, also south-east of the city. This is a more physically and technically challenging ride, for those who like a decent climb.

# Woodhill Mountain Bike Park

> More than 120 km of trails
> 1–2 days
> Skill level: all
> Map: Woodhill Mountain Bike Park map

Woodhill Mountain Bike Park is an ever-growing monster. It is professionally managed by Bikeparks and is Auckland's most popular riding spot by far. With such a huge population looking for a place to ride, Woodhill has truckloads of members and a lot of resources are put into the park. It's within Carter Holt Harvey's Woodhill Forest, an exotic pine plantation backing Muriwai Beach, and therefore has a distinctly sandy base. This means that the forest is good for riding year-round, rain or shine, and rarely accumulates surface water, but it also means gritty-sounding chains!

There is more than 100 km of riding in Woodhill on more than 50 trails. There are trails to suit all abilities and ages and a variety of terrain to satisfy all styles of riding. The trail system is clearly marked and course loops are colour coded for difficulty.

The terrain at Woodhill is undulating with no major climbs. Most of the trails are alongside reasonably mature pines with only low and non-invasive undergrowth. The trail surface is generally hard-packed sand and dirt with an overlay of pine needles. The forest is quiet and despite the hundreds of people sometimes riding in here you will often not come across others on the tracks.

 **The riding**

To get to Woodhill from central Auckland take the Northwestern Motorway (State Highway 16) to the end and turn left, staying on State Highway 16. Follow State Highway 16 past Kumeu for 12 km and turn left at the forest entrance, which is clearly marked. Drive up the sealed road and turn right into Boundary Rd. The car park is 1 km down this road.

The car park and base area at the forest has information, toilets, water, a small bike shop with on-site mechanic and a coffee and snack vendor. It is often a very social place, with dozens of riders milling around and chatting.

You must be registered to ride at Woodhill, either with an annual membership or a $5 day pass. There is a registration kiosk in the car park and an honesty system, if there is no staff member on site. The park gates are open 7am to 8pm in summer and 7am to 6pm in winter, with a late night on Wednesday until 10pm for night riding.

Woodhill Mountain Bike Park has an excellent website full of information with a downloadable trail map at www.bikeparks.co.nz; otherwise you can get a map from the registration area. The trail map has six suggested courses to start you off if you are new to Woodhill, ranging in distance from 6 to 25 km and catering for beginners, intermediate riders and XC-style riding, with more technical trails and a ride taking in the best of the forest's structures and stunts for more advanced riders. The map and marked courses are a pretty good place to start so, rather than providing any detailed instruction here, I suggest you just get a map, choose the most suitable track for your riding style and then head out on to it!

# Moumoukai Farm Track

17 km
1.5–2.5 hours
Skill level: recreational
Map: Hunua Ranges Regional Park map

The Hunua Ranges Regional Park south-east of Auckland is owned by the Auckland Regional Council and has three designated mountain-biking tracks: the Moumoukai Farm Track, which is described here; the Valley Loop Track, a linked collection of gravel roads; and the Mangatawhiri Challenge Track, which is best avoided unless you like a high proportion of uphill gravel and steeply undulating single track that's only semi-rideable.

The Moumoukai Farm Track and new River Track make up a 17 km loop, mostly on single track with a gravel road return route. It has short sections across farmland but ducks and swoops among native trees on well-made trails with a lot of little challenges. There are a couple of small river crossings where you will definitely get wet feet if there has been rain. This is generally a lovely, fun trail in the quiet setting of the tranquil Hunua Ranges.

 **The riding**

To find the mountain-bike trails in Hunua, first head to the township of Hunua, 50 km south-east of Auckland. From the township, follow Hunua Rd south-east for 6 km before turning left at Moumoukai Rd and following this all the way to the Mangatawhiri Dam car park, 14 km from Hunua. At the car park area there are toilets, a large basic camping area beside a creek, and a map board and track instructions for the ranges. There is no water here, despite the reservoir!

To get to the trails from the car park, head back up the gravel road but veer left at the first intersection, signposted with a bike symbol. From here the trails are marked the whole way with these symbols. Go around the gate and at 1.5 km from the start turn right and follow a four-wheel drive track to a right-hand turn into the marked single track (it's unnamed, but this is the new River Track).

At the 3 km point, after some very pleasant single-track riding, cross a small stream. Soon you will come out on to a road, where you turn left. Shortly after this, at a Y intersection, turn right and follow the symbol up the hill. Less than 100 m after this, turn right into the trail marked Moumoukai Farm Track.

Continue following the signs as this single track weaves through bush, crosses some open ground, dips into the creek and bumps over some rooty sections with a bunch of technical challenges.

At 9 km you will reach an intersection at the Lower Mangatawhiri campsite. Here you turn right on to a gravel road that is initially marked with horse-riding rather than biking symbols. Follow these to the end of the road, duck into the trees, cross the stream and pop out on to the gravel again and turn left. At 13.5 km you meet Mangatangi Hill Rd, where you turn left again at the horse-unloading area to head back to the car park 3.5 km away.

If you fancy another loop, head back into the River Track when you pass it.

# Waharau Ridge Loop Track

14.5 km loop
2–3 hours
Skill level: intermediate
Map: Waharau Regional Park Map

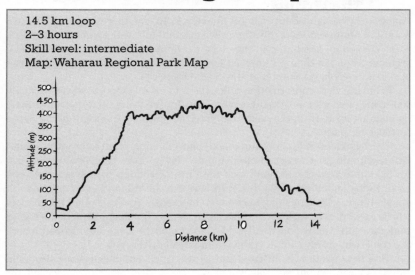

Waharau is another of Auckland's stunning regional parks and one of the few where there is some really sweet single track that you can legitimately ride. Waharau backs on to the Hunua Ranges and is on the Firth of Thames coast. It is surrounded by bush and sea, and with this blissful location there is plenty of opportunity for post-ride swimming and relaxing, and some pristine camping spots. You could easily make a great weekend of it just out of Auckland and feel as if you were hundreds of miles away.

There are numerous riding options here but as you will see by the landscape most include quite a lot of up. The ride described here is essentially the Waharau Ridge Loop Track with an added 'up and back' single-track excursion because it is the nicest single track around here and you are allowed to ride it! This little piece of trail is really the highlight of the Whakatiwai Ridge Track too, but riding it in this way cuts out the gruelling farmland uphill of that loop. There is also a shorter option here for a mixed-ability group, the 4.5 km Upper Link Track, a fun mix of single and four-wheel drive tracks.

 **The riding**

Waharau is 85 km south-east of Auckland. To get there from Auckland's Southern Motorway, take the Manurewa exit and follow the signs to Clevedon. From Clevedon, head around the coast towards Kawakawa Bay and Kaiaua. Waharau is on the right, 21 km past Kawakawa Bay. From the south, Waharau is also accessible via State Highway 2 at Maramarua.

From the visitor information office the track is marked the whole way by a red stripe on marker posts and several signs for the Waharau Ridge Loop. Start by heading away from the main road into the park, veering right towards the furthest car park.

The track starts by crossing a stile and climbing briefly across farmland before entering native scrub on a smooth clay surface. It climbs relentlessly for 3.5 km to a great viewpoint over the Firth of Thames, which is a welcome stop. Pretty much all of the track to here can be ridden if you are in good shape. If not, a little pushing may be on the cards. From this point the track is a little less rideable with some stairs and a steeper uphill gradient, but is cooler under the taller native bush. After 4 km you reach the ridge and turn left where the track widens into an overgrown four-wheel drive track.

This next section is all good fun as the track undulates along the main ridge. On a downhill section watch out for a right-hand turn marked for Whakatiwai (after 5.5 km) and head into this. This section of track is 2.5 km of lush, vine-surrounded, fun single track. It has been well maintained and has a partly gravel surface. When you reach the Whakatiwai Ridge Track, turn around and go back. Don't waste your elevation on the farm track! If you do plan to do the Whakatiwai Loop at any stage do it clockwise.

Enjoy the dense forest trail back to the main Waharau Ridge. Here you should really turn right and follow the main track all the way back to the car-parking area on a reasonably fun four-wheel drive track. However, if you prefer narrower and more technical downhill riding, you could turn left and head back the way you came up. This is definitely against the flow of traffic and therefore you must be super careful and keep your speed and control in check, all the way down the wild clay roller-coaster downhill.

**Coffee and food**

If you're heading north-west to Woodhill there are plenty of options for good food and coffee. Don't forget that the mountain-bike park does have its own café, so you will never be short of a pre-ride caffeine shot.

From the end of the Northwestern Motorway you will pass Blossoms Café, which is a good stop, as is Carriages Café in Kumeu. BeesOnline Honey Centre has very good food for a more upmarket experience and the kebab shop Miconose in Huapai is good, as is the Indian restaurant Curry Leaf in Kumeu. If you are not too stinky there is also a great selection of vineyards that do lunch.

Around Waharau, Clevedon is a good place to stop for coffee and With Relish is a fine choice. There is also the Clevedon Café, and the dairy sells ice creams. The Kawakawa Bay store is renowned for its ice creams, and past Waharau but worth the trip is the Kaiaua fish and chip shop. You might also like to stop in at the Italian Country Market on the Papakura–Clevedon Rd or time your trip for the Clevedon Farmers' Market on Sunday mornings.

 **Accommodation**

Camping is a good option for summer, especially near water. There is a campground at Muriwai Beach not far from Woodhill and another in nearby Helensville, near the hot pools. The winery area also has some B&B-style accommodation, as does Muriwai Beach.

In the south there is camping at Waharau and Hunua regional parks, where the riding is, and beautiful beachside camping at Tapapakanga Regional Park on the Firth of Thames. There is also accommodation at the Miranda Holiday Park next to the hot springs.

 **Things to do**

The closest beach to Woodhill is Muriwai, which stretches endlessly into the distance. It is a dangerous surf beach so swimming between the flags is definitely recommended. For a relaxing hot swim at the end of a day's riding at Woodhill head for Aquatic Park Parakai Springs near Helensville, which also has hydroslides.

To the south-east, the beaches on the Firth of Thames are all nice and safe but are tidal. A guaranteed good spot is Waiti Bay, east of Kawakawa Bay and off the main road. At low tide you can walk around to Tawhitokino, a sublime deserted beach. Waharau has a creek you can swim in and there are several nice beaches nearby (especially when the tide is in). If you are looking for a hot swim, then Miranda Hot Springs is not far south of Waharau.

 **Other rides**

Whitford Mountain Bike Park is another spot in the south-east that is popular and worth checking out if you are in the area. Try the Auckland Mountainbike Club website (address below) for details and a downloadable map.

---

### Contacts
**Woodhill Mountain Bike Park**: www.bikepark.co.nz
**ARC** (for information on all Auckland regional parks): 09 366 2000, www.arc.govt.nz
**Auckland Mountainbike Club**: www.aucklandmtb.co.nz

---

# Te Aroha and Bay of Plenty

Although Te Aroha and the Bay of Plenty are on opposite sides of the Kaimai Ranges, they are close enough to consider together in a weekend away. Te Aroha is a fantastic destination for its easygoing mountain-bike trail and divine mineral spa, and could provide a very relaxed weekend away in its own right. Just a scenic jaunt away, Tauranga has two areas of fun single-track riding on purpose-built tracks just a few minutes apart. The Bay of Plenty is well known for its excellent beaches and summer climate, and there is no shortage of places for a good coffee or more.

This weekend package is geared at families or groups of mixed abilities. The Te Aroha trail is suitable for all mountain bikers and would be a great place to bring kids. Likewise Summerhill Recreational Farm is aimed at all levels of riders but has technical aspects for more advanced riders to enjoy. They both also have walking tracks for any non-riding members of the group. Oropi is more suited to intermediate and advanced riders but in the small area and tight tracks others could also have fun. All three of these areas have relatively short rides, but your riding time could be lengthened by repeating fun trails. The proximity to more suburban pastimes will be an attraction to some groups.

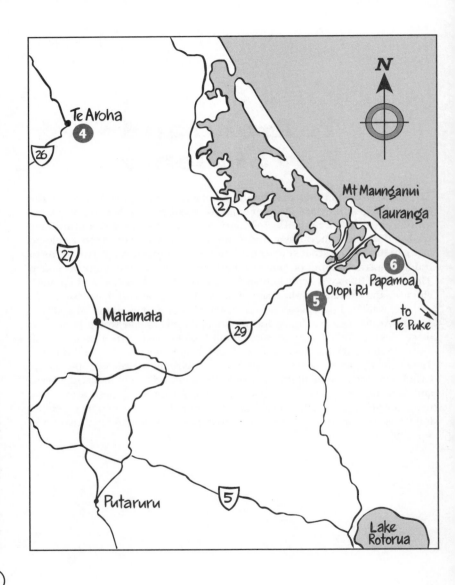

# Te Aroha Mountain Bike Track

> 12 km
> 1–2 hours
> Skill level: recreational
> Map: Te Aroha MTB Track map

The little town of Te Aroha is tucked underneath its namesake mountain where the Hauraki Plains meet the Kaimais. A very proactive destination, Te Aroha created a 12 km mountain-bike trail, which is a little treat. The track is well designed and built and has an easy gradient and a well-graded surface. It drains well, making it all-weather riding.

A trip to Te Aroha to try out the mountain tracks should be inseparable from the opportunity to test out the spa and mineral pools. The naturally hot soda mineral spas and the plush and immaculate facilities they are housed in are a serious attraction to the area and make Te Aroha a perfect winter riding destination. A map of the Te Aroha trails is available from the visitor centre in the main street, but you can't get very lost anyway.

 **The riding**

The trails start from the Te Aroha Hot Springs Domain off Boundary St. This is well signposted from the main street. From just inside the domain follow the mountain-bike symbols up a small rise on the left and then left again into the start of the tracks. You don't really need directions to ride here; you just follow the trail you start on and look for the bike signs and directional arrows at any intersections. The track is supposed to be one continuous loop with a few 'easy' and 'hard' choices in a couple of sections.

The single track is all on the lower reaches of Mt Te Aroha and faces out towards the town, providing you with a good point of reference when you can see it. There is essentially a small loop inside a much larger loop and the trails snake and wind along the side of the hill, often doubling back on themselves. The climbing is mostly in short sections and the gradient is reasonably easy.

There are a lot of swooping and flowing corners and the whole course is rideable for most people.

The trails are in a combination of low native bush, small open sections and a little bit of exotic forest. They are generally very well maintained, with no overgrowth. A lot of effort has obviously been put into keeping these tracks sustainable, with a surface of gravel, rock and playground matting and numerous small bridges. However, over time these trails have got better as the covering has bedded in to make a fairly smooth and fast solid surface.

Te Aroha is also a perfect night-riding destination as the trails have no serious obstacles, flow well, are close to town and reputedly have good glow-worms.

# 5

# Oropi Mountain Bike Park

> 1–3 hours
> Skill level: all
> Map: Oropi MTB Park map

Oropi is a sometimes forgotten gem on the outskirts of Tauranga. It is a small area in a valley with a tight collection of excellent single track. The area definitely has a downhill and jumps focus and this seems to be where most of the trail-building effort is being channelled. However, this shouldn't put you off heading here for a ride if you like a tightly crafted single-track lap with loads of corners. Just don't come looking for an extensive XC-style training zone. It is not a place for absolute beginners.

There is an excellent map of Oropi available from local bike shops, including Bike & Pack in Mt Maunganui. It is a weather-proof colour map and the $2.50 it costs is a fundraiser for the park.

 **The riding**

The car-parking area for Oropi is 3 km along Oropi Rd from its intersection with State Highway 29, and is on the right. There is a basic gravel car park (with evidence of a burned-out car), toilets, water and a bike-washing area. In early 2007 there was a sign for the Oropi Mountain Bike Park but no map board or trail instructions.

The layout of Oropi is easy. It covers both sides of a small valley with a stream running down the middle. At one end of the biking area is a water-pumping station and at this end is the only bridge across the stream. A gravel road runs from the car park down to the bottom of the valley but is not open to the public for cars.

To the left of the gravel road are the more extreme downhill trails into the valley. This is serious stuff and not for the kids. It's also where the exit trail comes back to the car park. To the right of the gravel road in the bottom of the valley is the jump park area known as the Pines. Above this area is a winding collection of sweet up and downhill trail. On the other side of the valley (by crossing the bridge) is another maze of trails suited to intermediate-plus riders, two small jumps areas and some extreme stuff.

So, head into the area via the entry track at the right-hand end of the car park (when looking away from Oropi Rd), follow this main trail down and, as you near the bottom of the valley, head right. Here you will come into the network of trails going both up and down on this side of the gully. They generally have a nice use of elevation so going up is fun too. The trails have great flow and swoop around the hard-packed surface with good berms and cambering. The trail marking here is by way of fluoro arrows painted on the trees that keep you hauling in the right direction (and these are directional tracks). At some point you will roll down into what is obviously a jumps area, full of doubles and tabletops with plenty that can be rolled over. On the low side of the jumps area is the trail to the bottom of the gully.

Head to your left up the valley to find the bridge across the river and follow the gravel track on the far side to the stream and another jumps area. Pass this a little way and a gravel track heads off on your left. A short distance up this the Switchback Trail climbs up, flattens off then descends, as you can guess, with a bunch of switchbacks forming a loop. Head back down the short gravel road and right into some single track that will head back up the valley, switching to both sides of a double track.

When you are ready to leave the valley head up the exit trail just along from the pumping station. This track is a fantastic example of how riding uphill can be a pleasure not a pain.

You really can't get lost here — you are easily able to keep your sense of direction and orientation — so just get in and have some fun. The only things to watch out for are the potentially damaging downhill trails if you don't mean to be there.

# Summerhill Farm

11 km + marked trail
Skill level: recreational

Summerhill Recreational Farm is a beautiful piece of private land generously made available for public use. It has a manager passionate about mountain biking, with years of experience, and significant resources have been put into trail development. The 130 ha recreational area of the farm is a mixture of mature exotic trees, remnant and regenerating natives, open pasture and an avocado orchard, and backs on to the Papamoa Hills Regional Park.

The farm is available for mountain biking, walking and horse riding. There is camping and several Mongolian-style ger are available for casual functions and as accommodation.

 **The riding**

The entrance to Summerhill is on Reid Rd, Welcome Bay, Tauranga. To get there, head along Welcome Bay Rd 10 km from its intersection with State Highway 29 or 3 km from the intersection with State Highway 2 (from Te Puke) and turn towards the hills. Follow Reid Rd 3 km and you'll find Summerhill Farm on your left. There is plenty of parking, an information kiosk, a toilet and, amazingly, a shower.

Admission to the park is by gold coin and users are asked to sign the visitors' book. The wooden kiosk has a track map, a key to the colour coding of marked trails and current trail information. Although the area is relatively new, things are changing all the time, with the felling of a significant section of exotic forest on the other side of the main road, and with the fast-expanding trail network.

At the start of 2007 the most popular mountain-bike track was the SRAM Track (marked with red). This rolling single track through native bush is well designed and built with tight corners and great flow. It has a few challenging sections but is aimed at XC-style riders of varying abilities. It's a 5 km loop that returns to the car park. The Truvativ Track (marked in black) forms a loop off the SRAM track and there is also the newly developed Jamis Track in the beautiful, rooty native area. There is a jumps area that you will pass when doing the whole loop. It has been built with some serious earthworks and a lot of enthusiasm. You could easily do a couple of laps of the lush native single track here for a ride of greater distance.

The additional riding heads out on to the farm to the east and follows a series of markers. The tracks out here aren't as well defined and are a mixture of narrow sheep and stock tracks and true cross-country riding. This is the place to go if you are looking for an extra fitness challenge or want to see the scope of the area and views from the farm.

There is an historic pa site on the high point just inside Papamoa Hills Regional Park. Although you are not allowed to bike up there it is well worth following the walking/biking track as far as you are allowed and then walking up to the summit. The views over the Bay of Plenty are spectacular and it gives you a good perspective of the layout of Summerhill as well.

 **Coffee and food**

The café in the Te Aroha Domain Cottage is a lovely place, has good food and coffee and the owner, Chris, is a mine of local riding knowledge. He has been riding for more than 20 years in the area and is happy to share some wider knowledge if you are looking for more local trails here.

From the riding locations around the Tauranga area, Mt Maunganui is probably the nicest (but busiest) place to head for a coffee and a snack or a meal. The beachside Marine Parade has a lot of good café options so take your pick. Maunganui Rd has the restaurants and bars.

If you want to get away from the young and silly, Tauranga has a lot of good spots too, with cafés on Devonport Rd and restaurants and bars on the Strand. Particularly worth a visit is the Fresh Fish Market, just around the end of the Strand on Dive Cres, which has fresh-off-the-boat fish and chips.

**Accommodation**

Te Aroha has a wealth of good accommodation options but can sometimes be busy. It seems the specialty is beautifully renovated B&Bs on the edge of the Edwardian-style domain, but they have everything else as well. The visitor information centre has the low-down.

If you are planning to drive through the Karangahake Gorge rather than over the Kaimais, there is a nice DOC campsite at Dickey Flat at the Waihi end of the gorge, with good swimming holes in the river. Heading out to the camping ground at Waihi Beach is a nice idea too. There is a lovely walk to Orokawa Bay from there.

For something completely different, stay in the Mongolian-style ger at Summerhill. It's probably not something you have done before but with comfy beds and a fireplace you might be tempted. It's a perfect adventure option for kids too. Contact Summerhill Farm in advance about this option.

There are camping grounds near Mt Maunganui and at Papamoa Beach but they are very busy in summer and best suited if you like a lot of teenagers! You can also camp just out of Tauranga at McLaren Falls, which is much more relaxed.

Tauranga and Mt Maunganui have loads of motels, backpackers and B&Bs.

**Things to do**

One of the main reasons to go to Te Aroha is for the hot pools. The fairly plush and excellent Spa Bath House in the Domain is where it's at. It's a good idea to book before you go for your ride, especially at weekends and when the weather is chilly. These pools are sensational. There is also an outdoor swimming pool and spa and kids' pool all in the domain. Te Aroha also has the world's only hot soda-water geyser. Be amazed.

Te Aroha has some great walking options if you need other ways to tire your legs. From the domain you can walk all the way up Mt Te Aroha in about 2.5 hours or to the Whakapipi Lookout in about 45 minutes. The nearby Waiorongomai Valley has many other great walks from 30 minutes to three hours. The DOC brochure *Te Aroha and Waiorongomai Walks*, available from the town's visitor centre, details all of these.

Te Aroha is particularly proud of its museum, housed in the beautiful exsanatorium in the domain. The whole domain is worth a wander for its beautiful surrounds and Edwardian buildings. There is also an historic buildings tour of Te Aroha, with a map available from the visitor centre.

Te Aroha and the Karangahake Gorge area have a rich mining history and a number of things to see. The Karangahake Gorge Historic Walkway is an interesting and scenic trip above the gorge's river and you are allowed to bike along it. Although not a challenging bike ride by any stretch, this is a fun way to see some history and a great view and is one to two hours return. The track would also be suitable for kids and walkers.

Over the other side of the Kaimais, Mt Maunganui Beach is a great place to swim. The surfing end is closest to the Mount and the safer swimming spots are on the far side of Moturiki Island. Papamoa Beach is also popular but the beach gradient is steeper both for swimming and strolling. Tauranga's beaches are on the harbour side so are not as picturesque and are much more tide-dependent.

## Contacts

**Te Aroha Visitor Information Centre**: 102 Whitaker St, 07 884 8052, www.tearoha-info.co.nz
**Te Aroha Mineral Spas**: Te Aroha Domain, 07 884 8717, www.tearohapools.co.nz
**Summerhill Farm**: (Karl Young), 07 542 1838, email info@summerhillfarm.co.nz

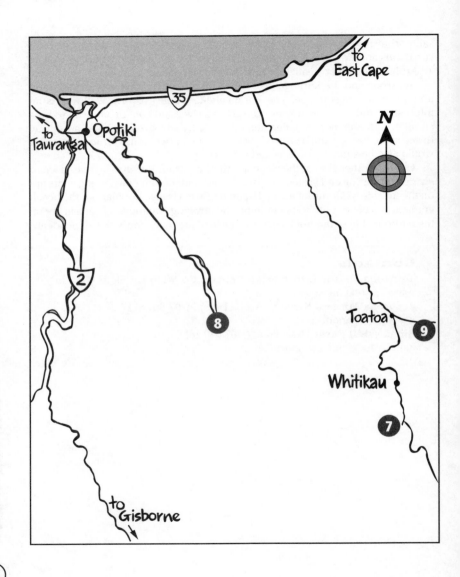

# Opotiki

People usually visit Opotiki for the coastline; stunning beaches, great fishing and because it is the gateway to the East Cape. Those are good reasons but the mountain biking is definitely another. It's not widely known about as a mountain-biking destination but a weekend at this place will convert you into a fan. This is an adventurous, amazing weekend away with a range of other recreational options, including beaches, and a guaranteed good coffee.

The recommended rides in this chapter are beautiful, remote, physically challenging and a lot of fun. The Pakihi Track is a stunning wild single track of perfect gradient and a great adventure for the confident and competent rider with good outdoor skills. The Te Waiti Track is a lovely easygoing single track suitable and fun for most riders but in a remote river valley. The Otipi Rd is an epic day out, only moderately technically challenging but very physically demanding, and for those who enjoy hills!

# Pakihi Track

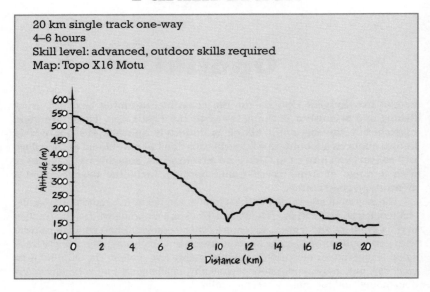

20 km single track one-way
4–6 hours
Skill level: advanced, outdoor skills required
Map: Topo X16 Motu

The Pakihi is a gem, hopefully about to get even better by a cut and polish from DOC. It is in the remote countryside of the Urutawa Conservation Area and runs between Motu Rd and Pakihi Rd near Opotiki. The Pakihi Track was originally a stock route between Opotiki and Gisborne and as such has a mellow gradient that, when ridden from the Motu Rd end is mostly downhill. However, don't be fooled into thinking this is a cruisy ride! The single track is narrow in parts, almost entirely on the edge of a significant drop and is prone to slips and fallen trees and other debris. It also has a crossing of the Pakihi Stream that is not safe when the river is in flood. This aside, the Pakihi is a classic adventure ride for those not afraid of heights, a narrow trail, a few obstacles and some remote terrain.

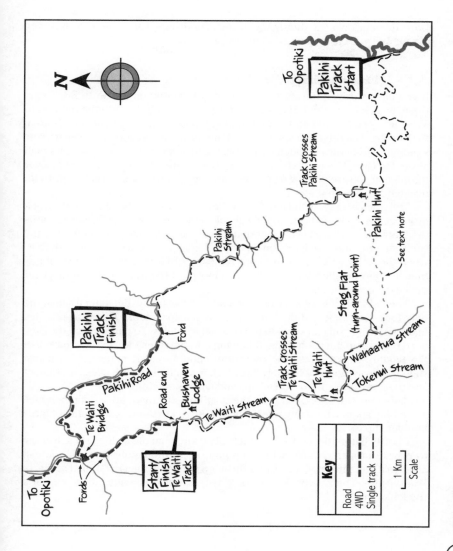

Key

Road
4WD
Single track

1 Km
Scale

N

Pakihi Track Start

To Opotiki

Track crosses Pakihi Stream

Pakihi Hut

Pakihi Stream

See text note

Stag Flat (turn-around point)

Pakihi Track Finish

Ford

Pakihi Road

Te Waiti Bridge

Road end

Bushaven Lodge

Te Waiti Stream

Track crosses Te Waiti Stream

Te Waiti Hut

Wahaatua Stream

Tokenui Stream

Start/Finish Te Waiti Track

Fords

To Opotiki

Don't do your own car shuttle if you can't get dropped at the start — it is way too far and will easily take 1–1.5 hours each way.

 **The riding**

If you have a driver, the start is 51 km out of Opotiki on the Motu Rd. To get there, head east on State Highway 35 for 12 km then turn off to the right on to Motu Rd, which you then follow for 39 km, passing the settlement of Toatoa, to the start. The drive is a spectacular but hair-raising experience. The narrow winding road passes through native bush and small farm blocks and sits high above the river. It is worth remembering that plenty of vehicles have gone over the edge. If you are coming from the south-east, it is possible to get to Motu Rd through Matawai and Motu.

The track is easy to find and follow. From the start the benched single track drops gently and winds along the side of the valley crossing streams towards the Pakihi Hut. There is some stopping and starting, mostly to climb over the small streams and any debris on the track. It may be worth checking with DOC when the track was last cleared but remember that foliage falls down at any time and any smaller stuff that you can move off the track makes it nicer for the next rider (or walker).

The Pakihi Hut is 10 km from the start and sits below the main track at the only fork. Head left and duck down to the hut for a look. This is also a nice lunch spot and you can swim in the river on a hot day. To continue on the ride, head back up to the main track, following it for another 1 km to the crossing of the Pakihi Stream. Cross the river with caution and re-enter the bush just slightly downstream. From here the track is similar but with a lesser gradient and there are a few more scree slips and narrow sections.

About another 4 or 5 km from the river crossing there are a couple of nice swimming spots with stony river beaches. At 16 km there is a significant large boulder slip to negotiate.

Shortly before the end of the track, at 20 km, is an old swing bridge leading to private property. Pass this by and pop out at the Pakihi Rd end. You can arrange to get picked up here, or a further 8 km down the gravel road at the Te Waiti bridge. The ride back to Opotiki is 23 km and is a slog at the end of a track like this.

# Te Waiti Track

12–20 km single track return
1.5–4 hours
Skill level: recreational/intermediate, outdoor skills required
Map: Topo X16 Motu

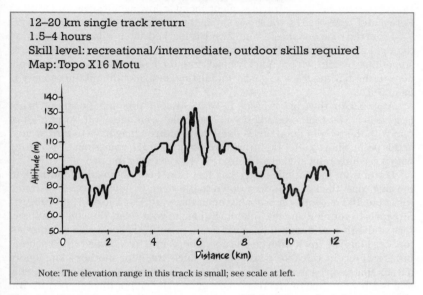

Note: The elevation range in this track is small; see scale at left.

This lovely single track (see map on page 35) is quite a find. It was poorly maintained for many years but was re-benched and drained by the former Bushaven Lodge proprietors and is now in near perfect condition.

From the Te Waiti Rd end to the Te Waiti Hut 6 km away the track rolls above the river through beautiful native bush, including dense groves of nikau, with river views and several pretty waterfalls. The gradient is minimal and there are few technical challenges. From the hut you can continue a further 4 km to Stag Flat on some more rooty and technical terrain before returning the same way.

**The riding**

To get to the start of the track from Opotiki take State Highway 2 towards Gisborne for 500 m then turn left on to Otara Rd. Follow this for 10 km until the road becomes gravel and then for a further 4 km to a single-lane bridge. Don't cross the bridge — travel straight ahead following the signs for Urutawa Forest and Te Waiti. The track is 4 km up this road.

From the road end the Te Waiti Track is marked and heads up the valley on the right side well above the river. The first short section is over grass and is sometimes overgrown but quickly heads into the lush bush single track. From here to the hut the track is gently undulating and smooth and the scenery is beautiful.

After 5.5 km the track crosses Te Waiti Stream. Although the stream is not large it is a 'wet-foot' crossing if you don't take your shoes off. After a lot of rain with the river in flood this is dangerous and you may have to turn around at this point. Shortly after the stream crossing, the track comes out to a clearing with a recently relocated eight-bunk DOC hut just over the rise.

If you want to continue on to Stag Flat from here, follow the foot track to the east (past the hut) and drop down to the river. Follow the river upstream for about 100 m (you will probably be in the water) to a fork. The Wahaatua Stream is to your left and the Tokenui Stream to your right. Take the right-hand fork of the river and stay in the river for 50 m until you see a sign on your left for Stag Flat. The track from here is not quite as well formed as the first section but is still readily rideable, with benched single track for another 4 km. Ignore a track that drops down to the river after about 20 minutes and continue. Stag Flat is a big flat area by the river and signifies the end of this lovely trail. You can then turn around and enjoy the whole thing in reverse.

Note: From Stag Flat it is possible to cross the river and carry your bikes for many hours over a connecting 'marked route' to the Pakihi Track. Some people managed to do this in 2007 in 11.5 hours but it's a big day out and is only for the extremely hardy. If you're tempted, do some investigation and take navigational equipment.

# 9

# Otipi Road

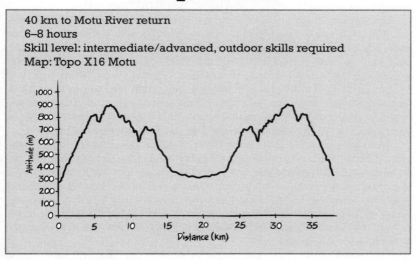

40 km to Motu River return
6–8 hours
Skill level: intermediate/advanced, outdoor skills required
Map: Topo X16 Motu

The Otipi Rd in the Raukumara Conservation Park was bulldozed through this rugged and remote country to investigate the hydroelectric possibilities of the Motu River. The idea was quashed by recreational and conservation opposition and the Motu River is now protected. The road has since been available for recreational use by walkers, bikers and four-wheel drive vehicles. Although the track is mostly wide enough for a vehicle, the natural erosion process has turned it into a rugged and sometimes technical uphill and downhill adventure ride all the way to the Motu River, with superb views.

 **The riding**

To get to the start of the track, head out of Opotiki in the same way as for the Pakihi Track by striking east on State Highway 35 for 12 km before turning

Opotiki

right on to Motu Rd. After 36 km you'll reach Toatoa and turn left on to Takaputahi Rd. Follow this road for a further 10 km until you come to a blue bridge and there is an obvious parking area by the river. The track starts on the opposite side of the river just under the Raukumara Forest sign and heads up into the bush. It may be easiest to ford the river on to the stony area to the right and then cut across the grass to the track. This is the Otipi Rd.

The track is 20 km up and over to the Motu River. The climb is relentless, going from 270 m to nearly 900 m in 7 km, but it's also challenging and fun negotiating the naturally sculpted track. There are several large slips that have tracks across them, thanks to DOC contractors, and there's a fallen tree or two. You can't go far wrong following the track as it is obvious the whole way.

For a full day's outing I would suggest going right over to the Motu River, stopping for lunch and having a swim if the weather is good. The Motu is a beautiful river and this is one of few remote access points. On a rare occasion you may see a group passing by on the four-day rafting trip down the river.

From the high point at 7 km the track undulates downhill for 14 km to the river. If you are not up to the full duration of the ride then turning around at the summit would still afford you some stunning views and track. We spotted a large stag on the track so keep your eyes open. The last few kilometres are much narrower as some foliage has overgrown the track and it is steeper. There will be some sections that require carrying here but it is possible to get right to the river. Be careful as a broken collarbone has been known to happen here and it's a long walk back.

The return trip from the river is back the same way. You will have a good idea what you are in for in terms of gradient, having just ridden down the track. The 7 km downhill back to the car after that is fast and bone-shaking even with good suspension, but damn good fun.

 **Coffee and food**

Opotiki is not known for its café and restaurant scene. However, it's worth mentioning the 2 Fish Café in the main street, which is excellent, with good coffee, fantastic muffins and some nice atmosphere. Other than that, Opotiki has a good supermarket on Bridge St (State Highway 2), a nice-looking fish and chip shop and the usual array of small-town pubs and coffee shops.

 **Accommodation**

Staying at Bushaven Lodge may complete the perfect weekend; it is quiet and relaxed and in a great location for riding. It's in a beautiful setting in an unpopulated valley right by the Te Waiti Stream and offers camping and self-catering lodge accommodation with full facilities. The lodge is also right at the start of the Te Waiti Track, and there are other walking track options from here from one hour to three days, as well as glow-worms nearby.

Opotiki also has a reasonable selection of motels, a nice-looking backpackers next to 2 Fish Café, several beach camping grounds and other countryside accommodation. The visitor information centre on the corner of John and Elliott streets has plenty of accommodation details.

 **Things to do**

The eastern Bay of Plenty and East Cape area have great beaches. Waiotahi is 6 km west of Opotiki and has good swimming, surfing and fishing. There is several kilometres of lovely sandy beach with shade under the pohutukawa trees and weekend beach patrols at the Opotiki end of the beach. Hikuwai Beach 3 km to the east is also a good safe swimming and relaxation spot and apparently has good surfcasting. River swimming in both the Te Waiti and lower Pakihi streams is good for a quick dip after a ride.

If you fancy some walking or tramping while in Opotiki there are plenty of good options. Te Urewera National Park is accessible via the Waimana Valley 45 minutes out of Opotiki, the Urutawa Conservation Area has walking tracks from the Te Waiti Valley, and the scenic Waioeka Gorge has various tracks along the road to Gisborne. The DOC office at the information centre has more information.

---

### Contacts

**DOC Opotiki office**: cnr John and Elliott streets, 07 315 1001
**Opotiki Visitor Information Centre**: cnr John and Elliott streets,
07 315 8484, www.opotikinz.com
**Bushaven Lodge**: www.bushhaven.co.nz, 027 375 7111

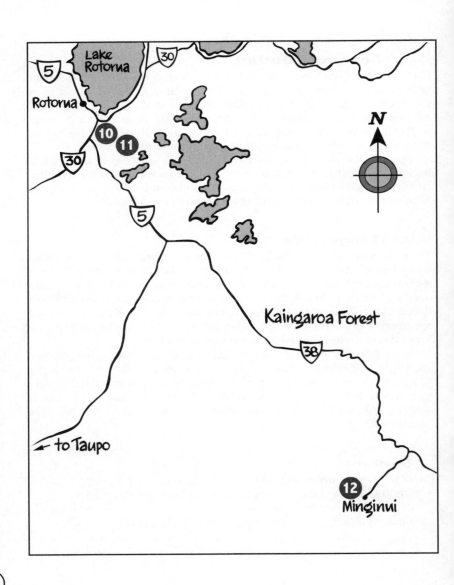

# Rotorua

**Riding in the Whakarewarewa Forest in Rotorua is an essential part of being a New Zealand mountain biker. It is often the first out-of-town trip for North Island riders and one that hooks them on weekends away riding. For South Islanders, it is a very worthy reason to be lured north.**

Few would dispute that the forest's extensive network of purpose-built single track is some of the country's best trails. The accessibility of the forest, the variety of levels catered to and the plethora of fantastic tracks make it a unique experience — and that is without even considering Rotorua's boiling mud and other intrigues.

Whakarewarewa truly has something for everyone, and is therefore an ideal place to bring groups of differing abilities or families. For competent mountain-bike riders, the specialty here is flowing benched single track with bermed and tight corners and excellent use of gradient in both directions. The forest is well mapped and easy to get around and is guaranteed to be enjoyed by anyone who goes there.

Whirinaki Forest has been a bit of a mountain-biking holy grail in this area, with very limited access, but DOC has recently opened a purpose-built track through the ancient forest, which is proving very popular for its scenery and as a day out from Rotorua. There are plenty of other activities such as walking, hunting and fishing in this area as well as in the adjoining Te Urewera National Park.

The Whirinaki track is a beautiful piece of wide single track accessible to most mountain bikers. Though it's not a technical challenge or very long, it can be ridden several times and it's worth doing for the unique landscape alone.

# Whakarewarewa Forest Inner Loop

21 km loop
2–3 hours
Skill level: recreational/intermediate
Map: Whakarewarewa Forest Mountain Bike Map

Whakarewarewa Forest is a privately owned plantation that has generous public access and 70 km of single-track trails to suit everyone. It borders the Rotorua District Council-owned Redwood Forest and has numerous access points. Most mountain bikers ride from the mountain-bike car park off Waipa Mill Rd. To find this, head south out of Rotorua on State Highway 5 for 3 km and it is clearly signposted on the left. At the car park there is water and bike-washing facilities as well as bike hire. A composting toilet is just inside the main trail system. The Long Mile Rd car park near the visitor centre is also a good starting place for some of the outback trails and riding on the northern side of the forest. The trails drain quickly so can be ridden in the rain.

There's a great map of the trails, created for the influx of people during the 2006 Mountain Bike World Championships. It's a good idea to pick one up if you have not done much riding in Rotorua — it's available from six local bike shops and the visitor information centre on Long Mile Rd. It costs $5 but is large, colourful and waterproof and is a worthwhile investment.

It is always tricky when you ride somewhere new to know where to go, even if you have a map. The Whakarewarewa Forest Mountain Bike Map has grouped the core network trails, which are nearer the car park, by difficulty, and suggested three additional 'outback loops' combining trails that fit well together and return to the same starting point.

What I've suggested here incorporates a large chunk of the forest's riding but is by no means all of it. The 'inner loop' covers the easier trails closer to the car park, most of which are classic original trails (with new names). The 'out-the-back loop' (see page 46) is a large helping of some of Rotorua's best more technical single track.

If you are new to riding in Whakarewarewa you should do a bit of a loop around some of the core trails in the forest. These are the less technically challenging ones closer to the car park, which have plenty of 'outs' from which you can head back to the car.

 ## The riding

Head into the forest from the main mountain-bike car park, over the bridge and then right into Tahi. Follow this until the Creek Track branches off to the right and then follow the winding and almost flat Creek Track until it comes out properly on to Nursery Rd. Turn left on to Nursery Rd and follow it back to the obvious T intersection with Pohaturoa Rd. Turn left down Pohaturoa Rd and very shortly afterwards hang another left into the single track now known as The Dipper. This is one of the original tracks in the forest and has become a bit of a highway but is still a lot of rolling fun. The trail winds back on itself a number of times through the big dipper and the infamous berm before finally coming out on to a gravel road.

Directly across the road (Bakers Hollow Rd) you will see a single track that is actually the end of the Tahi track you set out on. Avoid the walking trail starting just to your left. Head through Tahi and turn right on to Pohaturoa Rd. Continue along this road until the T intersection with Nursery Rd, turn left and ride up the hill to a four-way junction. Take a left at the top of the hill on to Radio Hut Rd. Just near the top of the rise (after 100 m or so) take the trail into the forest on your right marked Genesis. Follow this as it loops around clockwise and winds its way back to where you started. Duck back out on the dirt road, turn right and roll down the hill before heading left into the Challenge Trail. This is slightly more technical but is still an easy intermediate-level ride. There is also a bit more climbing in this track — good for your lungs. After the Challenge Trail, roll straight into Rockdrop. This is another step up on the technical stakes but remember that you can walk anything that doesn't take your fancy. Enjoy the challenge! When you hit Pohaturoa Rd head straight back into Rosebank for another little test before popping out right near the car park.

For beginner riders keep the loop to Tahi, Creek Track, The Dipper and back onto Tahi. This is straightforward and easy single-track riding that takes an hour or so and is suitable for families.

# Whakarewarewa Forest Out-the-back Loop

About 25 km
3–4 hour loop
Skill level: intermediate/advanced
Map: Whakarewarewa Forest Mountain Bike Map

This represents a fair share of the single-track riding on offer further away from the main car park. Plenty of extra side trips and loops are possible off this main loop so take your map. The riding is mostly intermediate level but is much more challenging at speed. Ride them a few times to get used to the flow while building up your speed.

 **The riding**

Start this loop from the Long Mile Rd car park (or mountain-bike car park if you wish). To get here, head up Tarawera Rd, turn right on to Long Mile Rd, drive past the visitor centre to the locked gate and park.

The road heading up into the forest is Nursery Rd. Ride around the gate and up. After about 500 m the road turns to gravel; continue up another 500 m and turn left onto Tokorangi Pa Rd. The climb continues — it will flatten off, go slightly down then climb again through the older exotic forest of gum and pine. After 20 to 30 minutes you will pass the walking track to Tokorangi Pa on the left. Shortly afterwards Tokorangi Pa Rd takes a 90 degree left turn but don't follow it — keep heading straight and up on what is now Katore Rd. Up a short hill will be a skid (deforested area), where you head right and slightly further uphill to Gunna Gotta. The entrance to Gunna Gotta is on your left. If you are going down the road you are on the wrong track and should turn around. This track is a combination of short little bits of up, followed by nice flowing down. It is much easier the faster you go.

the Mad Keen Mountain Biker's Road Trip

On the current map this track comes out on the road, where you'll turn hard right and ride for 300 m. Just before the sewage ponds, turn sharply left into the A-Trail. (Alternatively, you might find yourself coming out smack opposite the A-Trail, having followed a new piece of track. If so, ride on.)

Halfway around the A-Trail divides into easy and hard; take the easy — it is much more pleasant. Try doing no pedalling and using no brakes. After a small hill the track divides; take the straight/left option. The track will climb a little then lower on to a gravel forest track. Head left here and along to another skid. Follow the signs to Tickler. This is another faster-is-better track. The hard option in this track is only a roll over. Roll over the Wash Creek bridge and on up the hill. Cross Wash Rd, keep going straight and follow the trail uphill until you come out at what has become a bit of a hub for trails and roads. This is also the place to fill up with water.

From this junction, head up Direct Rd, named indeed for its directness. It is a lovely climb that can get very hot in summer and has all the views behind you. At the top is almost a T intersection. This gives you the option to turn left and along to Hot X Bun, or turn right and continue up Direct Rd and onwards with this loop.

If you decide to head towards Hot X Bun, turn left and continue up the hill and along. The trail starts on your left with a short climb and then some up and down initially. You will know when to put your seat down. This is a great ride that is probably the most challenging down trail on this circuit.

If you want to continue on — or you've finished Hot X Bun — go right at the intersection (staying on Direct Rd) and head uphill some more. At the next junction, with Hill Rd, go straight on to the trail (not marked on the map but signed as Frontal Lobotomy).

Frontal Lobotomy is not the bad experience its name suggests; it is instead a very nice up trail, with a slight sting. Exit the trail and turn left, go up the hill some more, past the gate and look out for the trail on your right. Put your seat down please.

Billy T is a masterful piece of trail building. After laughing your way through all of it, exit turning left then quickly right onto Chestnut Link. Ride the whole trail, not just down the middle, and you will come out on to a disused road (Chestnut Rd). Follow the tyre marks off to the left to Roller Coaster.

Right at the start of Roller Coaster you may be a little lost — the track is off to the left of the skid. Enjoy. Almost at the bottom is a slightly steeper section of trail with a T intersection; turn right (almost straight). (To the left are the

Pondy trails.) Ride on, crossing the road and then heading straight into Chop Suey. This is a short uphill grunt followed by some nice off-camber sections. Cross Hill Rd and head into Spring Roll. Keep going. Sweet and Sour is up next — sweet because it is good, sour because of the climb at the end! The trail ends back at the main intersection at the bottom of Direct Rd (aka The Hub). Look across the road from the end of the trail and you'll see Be Rude Not To.

Ah yes. Be Rude Not To. This is about as fast as Rotorua gets for a winding, beautifully cornered, no-brake downhill. At the first clearing in the track, head straight and fast on to the rest of the trail. At the second clearing, much bigger and defined, it is possible to continue on this trail a little further by heading left. It is easiest to exit here on to Wash Rd and turn left. Head along the gravel road looking for Pig Track on your right.

Pig Track is a really nice direct uphill. The trail gets slightly steeper and exits right on to a disused road. Continue straight ahead, right on the trail, up the nasty but short hill and then hard left onto Katore Rd.

For those who have parked at the mountain-bike car park, head down to the four-way intersection at the bottom of Katore Rd and turn left following Nursery Rd and then Pohaturoa Rd back to the car park (or any lovely combination of trails to take you to the same place).

For those who parked at Long Mile Rd near the visitor centre, I suggest turning left at the end of Pig Track, riding back down to the junction with Nursery Rd (about 600 m) then turning right on to Nursery Rd; the Exit Trail is on your right. This was one of the original jump tracks but has now mellowed into a very rideable downhill trail, a joy to finish off with. Ride the log, just don't try to roll over the no-roll-over drop! At the bottom you should be at your car.

Note: Southstar Shuttles operates a shuttle service from the Waipa Mill car park to Tawa Rd near Billy T on Saturdays, Sundays and public holidays only. Check out www.southstaradventures.com or be at the mountain-bike car park at 9.30am or 1pm. Each shuttle returns three hours later.

# Whirinaki Forest

16 km
2–4 hours
Skill level: recreational
Map: Whirinaki Mountain Bike Map

Whirinaki is an ancient beech forest and riding in it allows a rare look at a valuable ecological area. An excellent mountain-biking track was built through part of the forest in 2006 and opened to the public.

Technically the track is low-intermediate-level biking with some challenging sections. It is similar to the Rotorua trails in that it dries very quickly and is possible to ride in the rain.

 **The riding**

As a day trip from Rotorua, Whirinaki is about 90 km and takes around 90 minutes to drive. Follow State Highway 5 south-east from Rotorua, turning left on to State Highway 38 towards Murupara at Rainbow Mountain. Continue past Murupara and straight onto Ruatahuna Rd, which is now sealed but still very winding. Turn right to Minginui on Minginui Rd just after the bridge. Near Minginui turn right, cross the bridge and turn left up Old Fort Rd, following the signs. The car park for the ride is at the end of the road. Start from here.

The track is a loop and has one major vehicle access road through the middle of it, which you cross over twice. It is relatively easy to follow the loop, as it is signposted.

From the car park follow the trail for a nice little warm-up along flowing single track heading down. This is followed by a larger-than-expected across-and-up section; enjoy the log ride if you can. From here the track continues generally up with a perfect gradient until you reach the road. This is about one-third of the way around and is a sweet lunch spot with a table that is generally in the sun.

Turn right on to the road here (or left if you are looking for a quick exit back to the car) and head down then uphill for a short distance. Keep looking to your left along here for a single track; the turn-off is quite obvious. From here the gradient is gradually descending, potentially providing some high speed. The occasional water-races will provide entertainment along with the S-bend corners, narrow track and ditches on the far side. There is a shortish uphill section before you hit the road again; follow this along and into the track. You are heading into the final descent to the car park, saving the best until last — and unfortunately the end. But there is nothing to stop you doing it again!

It is not a bad idea to have a trail map but you don't need one — there is a great map at the start of the trail and with these instructions it is hard to get lost. Maps are available from the DOC office at Murupara or you can download the PDF from: www.vorb.org.nz/images/attach/bike_brochure_low_res.pdf

 **Coffee and food**

Rotorua has a pretty good selection of coffee, food and drink outlets. The most popular choice for cool mountain bikers is Zippy Central (1153 Pukuatua St).

Other good choices are Lime (corner Fenton and Whakaue streets), Fat Dog Café (1161 Arawa St) and Capers Epicurean (1181 Eruera St). For an ice cream, try the local institution Lady Jane's Ice Cream Parlour (Tutanekai St, near the lake). The café at the Outdoorsman Headquarters on Tarawera Rd often does a good coffee too.

 **Accommodation**

Rotorua has loads of accommodation to suit all budgets from plush hotels and lodges to backpackers and camping grounds. The choice is yours. You can get some good deals on www.wotif.co.nz.

 **Things to do**

Swimming in Lake Rotorua is not the best choice with so many other stunning options. However, you can enjoy a dip in the lake near Hamurana at the northern end, or near Holdens Bay on the south-eastern shore.

The better spots are the Blue Lake (Tikitapu), Lake Okareka or at the landing on Lake Tarawera (where there is also a very picturesquely situated café). Don't try the Green Lake (Rotokakahi) as it is tapu and thus out of bounds for swimming and fishing.

If you are after one of the many hot-swim options there is the Polynesian Spa (on Hinemoa St), a popular modern pool complex on the lake edge. If you like things a little more rustic and free then you could try the naturally thermal Kerosene Creek (22 km south-east of town on State Highway 5; turn left at the signpost). The Secret Spot is not very secret these days, but is a great spot where a hot and a cold river come together into a multi-temperature pool. This is about 24 km south of Rotorua on State Highway 5. Pass the sign for Waiotapu Thermal Wonderland and turn left after 500 m. Drive down this gravel road and you come to a small bridge. Park here and follow foot tracks down the bank on your right into the steamy stream. Bring a torch if it is dark.

The Luge is a popular extra-adrenalin activity to top off a Rotorua weekend. It is operated by Skyline Skyrides on Fairy Springs Rd. You ride up to the course in the gondola and fang down on a little trolley. Great fun.

Rotorua abounds with 'culture' in the true tourist interpretation of the word. There are plenty of opportunities to see bubbling mud and model villages if you want, a lot of which is actually quite interesting if you could just get away from the tourists!

## Contacts

**Bike Culture**: (servicing experts): 1133 Pukuatua St, Rotorua, 07 343 9372

**Redwoods Visitor Centre**: Long Mile Rd, Whakarewarewa, 07 350 0110

**Rotorua Mountain Bike Club** (for updated track information and news): http://rotorua.mtbclub.org.nz

**DOC Area Office Murupara (for Whirinaki)**: Main Rd, Murupara, 07 366 1080

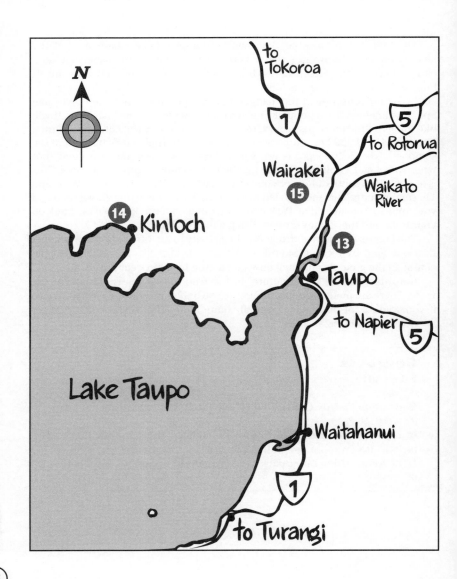

# Taupo

**Everyone seems to have been to Taupo, but not everyone has visited because it is a fantastic mountain-biking destination, and growing more and more fantastic. Bike Taupo are responsible for almost all the trails in the area, and provide the advocacy, planning, maintenance and funding of these. They are doing a sterling job, and Taupo is a very worthwhile weekend riding destination indeed.**

Taupo has all the trimmings of a popular tourist town and you are sure to find paua souvenirs and possum-fur gloves for sale on numerous street corners. It also has plenty of great cafés, decent pubs and all the amenities you could want. There is more than enough beautiful scenery, hot and cold swimming, all the expensive extreme sports you can think of, fishing and golf if you like it and any type of accommodation you could want.

This weekend away offers a fine selection of single-track rides that will be loved by all mountain bikers. The beautifully formed trails provide options for beginners to highly skilled riders and you could have a great social weekend away with a group or a family. The return ride to Aratiatia Dam can be taken as a two-hour blast or a leisurely, scenic day out and is suitable for all riders. The Kinloch ride is short and has some testing little climbs and technical challenges but nothing that can't be walked if required. It is also a perfect excuse to stop at the café L'Arte and see another side of Lake Taupo. And then there is Wairakei Forest, which could provide a weekend of great riding in itself. With fun, well-marked and graded trails, it has a lot of good stuff for everyone's taste and ability, and you can ride single track from town to get there.

# Rotary Ride To Aratiatia Dam

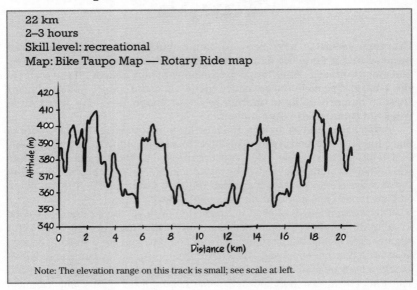

22 km
2–3 hours
Skill level: recreational
Map: Bike Taupo Map — Rotary Ride map

Note: The elevation range on this track is small; see scale at left.

It would be hard not to love this ride. It is an uninterrupted fun, flowing single track beside a river with stunning scenery. It can be ridden by all levels but is still a real blast for highly skilled riders. It's well constructed and maintained and all just an easy ride from a good café.

 **The riding**

To get to the start of this ride from the centre of town, ride or drive down Spa Rd and turn left into County Ave. Head through Spa Park to the end of the road where the car park is. From here you will see a sign for the 'Rotary Ride' to Huka Falls.

From the start in Spa Park the ride is 11 continuously lush kilometres of single track to the Aratiatia Dam. Initially the track passes through Spa Park before hitting the pumice-based track just out of sight of the mighty Waikato River. The overall height change on the ride is less than 60 m but there is plenty of opportunity to enjoy some fun descents with fast flowing corners. At several points the track is divided into up and downhill traffic, reducing anxiety and hopefully the crash rate and increasing the guiltless pleasure.

Much time, money and effort has been put into Taupo's mountain-biking showpiece and the result is a stunning track. The trail is well built and has withstood some 18,000 pairs of wheels passing over it during the Taupo Day-Nighter. It is being continuously maintained and various strategies are in place to help deal with the effects of erosion.

The track is easy to follow. You can't really get lost if you stay on the main trail and follow the signs to Huka Falls and then to the Aratiatia Dam. The first section of the track is further from the river and part of the trail backs on to some private forestry. There is a short darker section through a pine plantation where the track widens; look out for arrow markers on the trees in here. The whole 4 km or so to Huka Falls is all undulating goodness above the river. The trail is a lot of fun and rideable for people of all levels of ability and the views of the river are marvellous.

When you get nearer to Huka Falls, follow the MTB Rotary Ride signs carefully, as the trail briefly merges with the walking-only track. You can pop out to the main viewing areas for the falls here, and whether you have seen the falls before or not they are always worth a look (and a bit of head scratching about the people who kayak over them!).

Downstream of the falls the water is a beautiful colour and the scenery continues to be stunning. There are a lot of good viewing spots on the earlier part of the 7 km section to the Aratiatia Dam before the trail drops into trees well above the river. Eventually, after a long gradual downhill, you come out on to an access-type road and then the dam car park. This is the end of the trail, where you turn around and enjoy the whole thing in reverse.

The Aratiatia Dam is opened and closed on the Waikato River on a regular basis during the day. It's worth timing your ride to arrive for the opening. In summer the gates are opened at 10am, 12pm, 2pm and 4pm and you can watch the flooding of the river below the dam. You probably don't need to watch the whole 30 minutes but it is a good spot for a rest and snack before the ride back.

# Kinloch–Kawakawa Bay

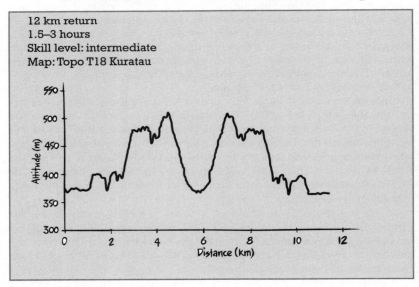

12 km return
1.5–3 hours
Skill level: intermediate
Map: Topo T18 Kuratau

I have always thought this ride to be an under-appreciated gem. And for those who need a change from bike parks, this out-and-back ride on the north edge of Lake Taupo will be a delight.

## The riding

The ride starts at Kinloch, a sleepy little village 19 km from Taupo. Head north out of Taupo on State Highway 1 and the turn-off is signposted just over the bridge. (Kinloch will soon be home to a massive new Jack Nicklaus signature golf course with plush bar and restaurant.) Once in Kinloch, follow your nose to the lake edge where the shop and parking area are.

From the car park head right (west) along the lakefront, initially pedalling then walking along the foreshore for about 200 m. The track to Kawakawa Bay is clearly marked from here with a DOC sign and you can't get lost. The track undulates over several rises and there is a shallow stream crossing (worth taking shoes off for if you don't want to ride it), a steep staircase to carry up, a couple of wooden bridges and a rocky uphill before you come to the highest point above Kawakawa Bay. The track is almost entirely in native bush and has some root and rock obstacles that are fairly easy to negotiate. It is beautiful single track, padded down by years of foot-only traffic, which swoops around lovely curves before coming out into the open for stunning views down the length of the lake from 500 m elevation. From here the descent is fast and furious, or you can ride with caution if you are not so confident. The beach at Kawakawa Bay is a little thin on foreshore but it's long and in summer is worthy of a picnic or a swim at the least.

When you have done with Kawakawa Bay return the way you came and be prepared to walk back up some of that lovely down unless you are feeling pretty strong. I always appreciate that when you ride a track in both directions you get double the pleasure and two completely different experiences, and I like to think of it in these terms rather than as retracing your steps. A lovely little bike ride.

# Wairakei Forest Trails

Up to 70 km
1–2 days
Skill level: all
Map: Bike Taupo — Wairakei Forest Track System

Huge development of trails in the Wairakei Forest in the past couple of years has re-hatched the area around Craters of the Moon as a major riding destination. The area is full of hand-made, mountain bike-specific flowing single track. The trails have a natural feel to them and due to the pumice base drain well for year-round riding. The trails link together, accurately follow the

Taupo

available map and are colour coded for difficulty, providing suitable riding for all levels.

 ## The riding

To get to the forest trails head north out of Taupo on State Highway 1 for about 5 km. A good place to park and start from is the Hub Café at Helistar. This is opposite Karapiti Rd and has a large helicopter outside. You can also easily get here by bike along the Spa Park to Huka Falls section of the Rotary Ride, or by ducking into the new Redwoods Track, which is on the left off Huka Falls Rd, and then taking the single track from the Huka Falls car park to the Hub Café.

Taking a map of the trail system with you is always a good idea, though there is good signage and a map board. You can download a map from www. biketaupo.org.nz or buy a waterproof one from the café, the Taupo information centre or any of the town's bike shops.

From the Hub Café you should ride through the tunnel under State Highway 1. The track to this tunnel is just off to the left of the café, right next to the developing 'bike fence', and is a sweet new trail. On the other side of the highway you will pop up just opposite Inward Goods, the entry track that leads you into the heart of the trail system. The trails in here tend to be tight and winding but flatter than the rest of the forest and are a good warm-up. Follow Inward Goods and Piker or Tourist Trap across this section of forest to the car park.

From here there are numerous options of where to ride and anything from one to six hours, or more, is possible.

Intermediate-level riders and above can get started with a nice loop by heading into the Lake Hire Link track and hanging a left up Tank Stand. This continues upwards and turns off to the Ground Effect Grinder, getting a bit steeper. Near the top take Buzzard out to the road and then head into the Young Pines Trail. When this loops back to a trail hub, cross over the road, go up the hill and into the Coaster or Walter's Wiggles for some great fun on your way back to the link track and car park.

If you are looking for a bigger effort then work in the Outback loop. There is plenty of climbing here but it all comes back down too, in some great fun trails.

**Coffee and food**

Taupo has an extensive selection of cafés and all other types of places to eat and acquire food. The classic stopping point to fuel up in Taupo is the Replete Café in Heu Heu St, which has good coffee, an extensive selection of great food and good stuff to take away on your riding trip. Many people find their kitchenware shop quite a distraction too. Others worth a mention are Zest Deli Café in slightly more suburban Rifle Range Rd, Flax Café in Horomatangi St, and the Jabies Doner Kebab shop, also in Horomatangi St.

An essential stopping point on the way to Kinloch (or a worthwhile trip purely to eat, drink and relax) is the café L'Arte, with sculpture garden, on Mapara Rd near Acacia Bay. The café has sensational food and good coffee and is licensed. It is in a lovely country environment and with the clever concrete creations this place is a real treat.

Taupo has several supermarkets, the most obvious being the open-late Woolworths on the corner of Spa Rd and Tongariro St.

 **Accommodation**

As such a major tourist destination, Taupo has accommodation options coming out its ears. Any quick search of the internet will leave you perplexed by the choice but there is something for most budgets. If you are looking for the best free camping option close to town it is probably Reid's Farm, a picturesque reserve on the banks of the Waikato River. It's a legitimate free camping spot administered by the Taupo District Council and open from the start of October to the end of April. It has only basic toilet facilities. You will find it off Huka Falls Rd.

 **Things to do**

Again, as such a major tourist destination there is plenty of sightseeing to be done especially if you are prepared to pay! Huka Falls shouldn't be missed but this can be taken in as part of the Rotary Ride or on the trip out to Wairakei. The Craters of the Moon walkway is a great way to get in among some thermal activity and, with admission by donation, it is cheap and much more low-key compared with the other thermal sights. You can't take your bike in here. Just being in the Taupo area is a sightseeing experience and the stunning view down the lake to Tongariro National Park is one of the best sights.

The area surrounding Taupo has a lot of other recreational opportunities. As well as the great mountain biking, the area is promoted as a road-cycling destination and the 160 km lake circumnavigation is a long but good ride.

There are many short and long walks around Taupo if you need to give your backside a rest but still get out and do something. There are tracks around the Huka Falls area, and the Huka Falls to Aratiatia Dam track is open to walkers as well as bikes. There is a nice lake-edge path heading south from town to Five Mile Bay and you can wander in Spa Park. If you want to get out of Taupo for a real tramp there are good options too and the visitor centre has information and DOC brochures.

With so much water around, Taupo is a sweet spot for swimming. Luckily there are some hot-water options because the lake is not renowned for its warmth! Plenty of people swim close to town or near the exit of the Waikato River; both Acacia Bay and Kinloch are nice and less busy spots.

If you are looking to warm up or relax your well-pedalled legs, some thermal water will help. Otumuheke Stream in Spa Park is a naturally hot stream and it's free. It can be a busy wee spot but is close to town and easily accessible. From the Spa Park car park head across the large grassy field and find the stream under a walking bridge flowing into the Waikato. Butcher's Pool just out of Reporoa (between Taupo and Rotorua) is a classic free hot pool on farmland that has been well looked after. It is signposted off Broadlands Rd, about 2 km from Reporoa.

If you are looking for something a little more commercial you could try the AC Baths towards the end of Spa Rd, or DeBretts Thermal Resort at the start of the Napier–Taupo Rd, which is always nice and now has rather swish accommodation, as well as tent sites.

## Contacts
**Bike Taupo**: www.biketaupo.org.nz
**Taupo Information Centre**: Tongariro St, 07 376 0027, www.laketauponz.com

# Turangi

**Turangi, at the southern end of Lake Taupo, is a funny little town. Built as a service town for a hydroelectric power station, it is increasingly a tourist destination due to some exceptional recreation around the area. Most people know Turangi for its access to Lake Taupo, its world-famous trout fishing, river rafting, hot springs and for its incredibly busy petrol station. Several essential mountain-bike rides around the area make it an important destination for those who appreciate fine single track.**

Turangi is a great place if you want to avoid the hustle and bustle of Taupo and get into the wilderness a little further. There is fantastic free camping, great swimming, hot pools and hiking. Turangi is also on the doorstep of the Kaimanawa Forest Park, Pureora Forest Park and Tongariro National Park.

The riding in this part of the country is lush and varied. The predominant beech forest provides the perfect riding surface with just enough roots and a delicious cornflake-like ground covering. Tree Trunk Gorge is a classic ride that has been enjoyed since the country's mountain-biking pioneer times. Some recent track improvements have tidied things up and added the icing on the cake to the end of the ride. Be prepared for some spectacular scenery. The Waihaha Hut ride is a more technical ride for intermediate to experienced mountain bikers and is a fantastic little adventure. It would have to be one of my very favourite day rides in the north. As a little scenic something or a ride for the whole family, the Tongariro River Walkway is a fun flat cruise along the riverside in Turangi. Not challenging, not long, just nice.

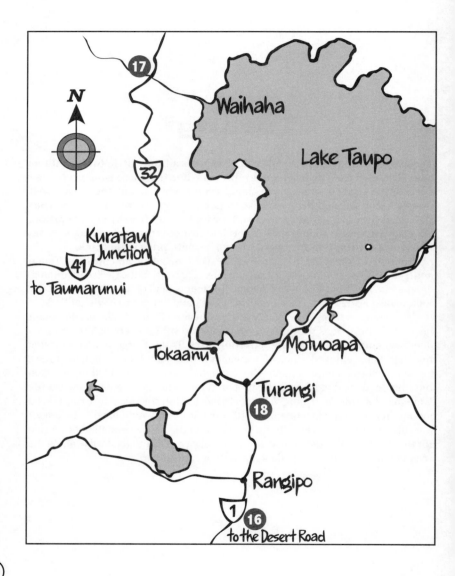

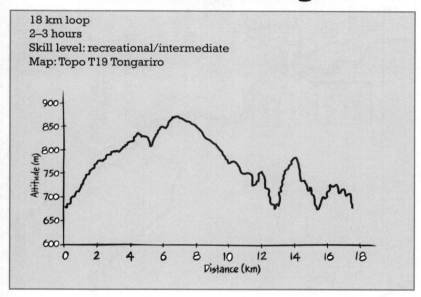

## 16

# Tree Trunk Gorge

18 km loop
2–3 hours
Skill level: recreational/intermediate
Map: Topo T19 Tongariro

Tree Trunk Gorge could best be described as a lush little loop that would serve well as an introduction to 'real trail' mountain biking. It takes you out, loops around and delivers you back to your car while taking in some amazing scenery and trail.

It's a small taster for beech forest that will most likely leave you reading through this book looking for more and a perfect little 'hello' to what is on offer on this side of the Kaimanawa Forest Park. It is suitable for most mountain bikers but technical sections may have to be walked by less experienced riders.

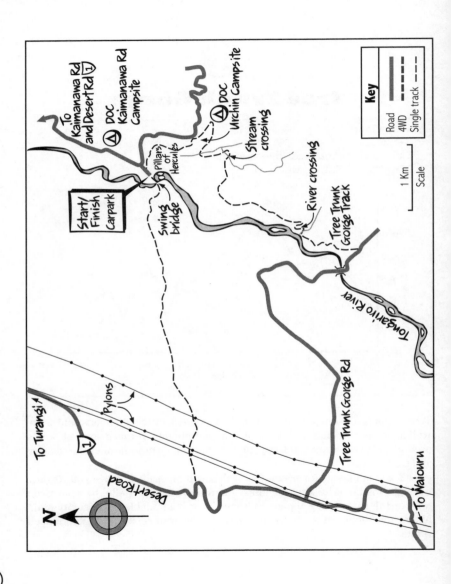

**Key**
Road ———
4WD – – –
Single track - - -

1 Km
Scale

N

To Turangi
1
Desert Road

To Kaimanawa Rd and Desert Rd 1
DOC Kaimanawa Rd Campsite
DOC Urchin Campsite
Pillars of Hercules
Stream crossing
Start/Finish Carpark
Swing bridge
River crossing
Tree Trunk Gorge Track
Tongariro River
Pylons
Tree Trunk Gorge Rd
To Waiouru

**The riding**

This loop ride can be started in several different places. The way I have described it has it finishing with a sweet single-track descent back to your car.

From Turangi drive south on State Highway 1 (Desert Rd) for 15 km before turning left into Kaimanawa Rd. At 18.5 km turn right at a DOC sign for the Tree Trunk Gorge Track (among other things). At the next Y intersection head right towards the Pillars of Hercules and follow to the road end and car park, at 20km. On the way you will pass the DOC Kaimanawa Rd Campsite, a great little possie for free camping. There are also several nice sites down by the river further along Kaimanawa Rd.

From the car park the trail to the Desert Rd is clear. Cross the new swing bridge looking down through the foliage to the Pillars and then follow the track for 4.7 km to State Highway 1. This former four-wheel drive track is fast becoming single track as a new line is forged up the middle and manuka grows in from the sides.

At State Highway 1 turn left on to the main road and be careful to ride single file as this is a busy, winding road. At 6.7 km from the start turn left again into Tree Trunk Gorge Rd. Coast down this sealed road until you reach a bridge with spectacular gorge views at 11.7 km. Shortly after this, the Tree Trunk Gorge Track is clearly marked on your left.

From this point the trail is sweet single track all the way back to your car. Yum! It is a combination of a slightly wider pumice surface and tight winding beech forest with roots and technical challenges for everyone. At 13.2 km there is a wet-foot river crossing and a new piece of trail clearly signposted with an orange marker. Following this there is another small stream and several wooden bridges, only just handlebar width wide. Around the 16 km mark the track runs beside and then crosses a stream to the left. Shortly after this you will pop out at the Urchin Campground (another sweet free camping spot).

From the end of this section of trail turn right and then immediately left into the Pillars of Hercules track. This has only recently been opened to mountain bikes so take care of this lovely trail. Don't skid too much and watch out for walkers. This is 2 km of lovely beech-cornflake covered trail with a couple of switchbacks just before the end to top things off. Sensational.

# Waihaha Hut

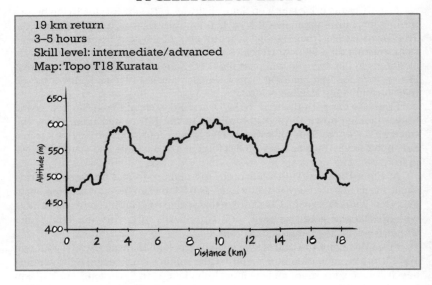

19 km return
3–5 hours
Skill level: intermediate/advanced
Map: Topo T18 Kuratau

Commonly known as 'Laughing Water', the Waihaha Track in the Pureora Forest Park is a fantastic ride providing a wonderful variation in terrain over a short distance. It is technical in parts with numerous small challenges for intermediate and advanced riders. For those who have never been hut-riding it is a perfect introduction, and a small-scale wilderness adventure. It could also be a perfect first overnight ride and is a lovely walk for non-riders in your group.

 **The riding**

The ride starts from State Highway 32 (the Lake Taupo western access road).

From the north, it is 40 km south of Whakamaru, where a bridge crosses the river at the bottom of a long dip. From the south the car park is 28 km along State Highway 32 from Kuratau Junction. The closest supplies can be found at the Tihoi Trading Post, 10 km north of the track.

The track starts on the opposite side of the road from the parking area (where you are advised not to leave valuables and to leave everything else out of sight). There is a clear sign to Waihaha Hut and just inside the track is a drop box for deer jaws. The track is obvious the whole way to the hut and you can't get lost as long as you find the track again after the one major fallen tree.

From the start the trail goes through grassy single track and lowland scrub and crosses a series of small bridges. It follows relatively closely beside the Waihaha River until it crosses the Pikopiko Stream on a swing bridge. After the swing bridge there is a short section of riding and then the track deteriorates somewhat as it climbs up to a great viewpoint. This will be a push or carry most of the way up but it isn't too far. It used to be a very tricky ride down but seems to be becoming increasingly rideable as water erosion forms ruts to the side of the old stairs.

From the obvious viewpoint you can get back on your bike for some challenging uphill riding. The track goes up and over a high point in lush native bush before descending to some grasslands. The fun track scoots across the grassy area and some pumice ruts before rising up and traversing above the river. About 6 km from the start and just after a wooden bridge is a point where you can nip down to the river for a swim or at least take a look.

The track then heads back into the beech forest for a bit, comes out above the river again (to a nice view of a waterfall). At this point you are about two-thirds of the way (in time, not distance) to the hut. The track then has a technical rooty forest section before arriving on a slight downhill to the hut.

The new Waihaha Hut has 10 bunks and is rather palatial. It is a perfect lunch spot with a sunny deck and has plenty of room and light inside. If you are planning on staying the night you need a DOC hut pass or tickets. There is a stream just opposite the hut for a wash and it is a great spot to relax in. The hut is usually supplied with coal.

To get back to the car you head out the same way you came in. It feels much more of a downhill on the way back but the elevation loss is only 130 m or so. It is definitely faster and a lot of good fun. Enjoy!

# Tongariro River Walkway

10 km return
1–1.5 hours
Skill level: recreational
Map: Topo T19 Tongariro

The Tongariro River Walkway is a relaxing little jaunt along the riverbank. This is an internationally acclaimed trout-fishing river and can be busy. The walking track beside the river, which is open to bikes, is a gradient-free roll around on single track to stretch your legs in a lovely spot. It is suitable for all riders.

 **The riding**

The easiest place to start this track is at the Major Jones footbridge that crosses the Tongariro River at the end of Koura St. To get here, head down Arahori St (opposite the petrol station on State Highway 1), turn right into Taupahi Rd and left into Koura St.

There are numerous foot tracks for anglers and other walkers in this area. Bear in mind that serious people are fishing here so avoid coming right down to the pools as much as possible and keep noise at a reasonable level. This is also a popular walking area so take care and have a cruisy ride so you don't scare any pedestrians.

The main track beside the river is on the far side. This heads upriver to the Blue Pool. This is the longest stretch of trail and rolls beside the river for about 5 km. It passes through native bush and along the edge of farmland. There are good views of the calm pools and wee rapids. If you keep your eyes peeled you may even see a trout. You will pass the Red Hut footbridge not long before the dead end at the Blue Pool. From here you turn around and meander back the way you have come.

Other sections of trail are worth exploring but most are dead ends that require you to retrace your pedal strokes. The near side of the river at the

Major Jones footbridge has tracks that go both left and right but do not extend as far down the river as the main track. These are both worth a look.

 **Coffee and food**

Turangi is not recognised for its fine dining and you will have better luck with fish and chips. I hate to have to say that I have not yet found a good coffee here either, which is disappointing and will hopefully change soon. Bring your stove-top espresso and a camping stove and cook up your own.

 **Accommodation**

Like all towns that attract a passing tourist population, Turangi has reasonable accommodation options from backpackers to motel and lodge-style accommodation. Camping is the superior option around these parts and the edge of the Kaimanawa Forest Park has several great spots. DOC has free basic campsites near the start of the Tree Trunk Gorge ride. These are the Kaimanawa Rd Campsite, the Urchin Campsite (see ride text for locations) and several lovely sites along the river before the underground powerhouse. To get to these sites head straight ahead where you would have otherwise turned right to the Tree Trunk ride and follow your nose and/or signs to the river on your left. These are all back-country sites with no facilities except fire pits and you should bring your own water. The Kiko Rd campsite at the end of Kiko Rd, 10 km north of Turangi, is a similarly rustic spot and there is a loop of trail that you can ride here. The temptation to ride the rest of the lush single track may prove too much for mortals.

 **Things to do**

For a cold dip (and Taupo is often quite cold), Stump Bay, 7 km north of Turangi, on State Highway 1, is a nice safe swimming area with a pumice/sand beach. Kuratau, 15 km away on State Highway 41, is a good spot to access the lake if you want to spend a bit more time. Tokaanu Thermal Pools just out of Turangi are excellent and clean, a great post-ride relaxation spot. There is also a little thermal walk around this area and a BBQ site.

If you are not tired enough from riding, want something a little different, or if you get waylaid by some rain, try the indoor climbing wall at the Extreme Backpackers in Ngawaka Pl, which also has a café.

Make sure you pause long enough near the start of the Tree Trunk Gorge ride to have a good look at the spectacular scenery. Many people come just to gaze.

It is possible to make your way down to the upstream side of the Pillars of Hercules (100–150 m along from the bridge, down the steep bank) and swim through. It's very nice, just not in the rain.

If you have a fascination with fish or are a keen angler then a visit to the National Trout Centre, 4 km south of Turangi on State Highway 1, may be in order.

 ## Other rides

At Pureora Forest Park, DOC is very progressive in its approach to mountain biking. Staff are working on a trans-Pureora traverse track and upgrading and linking a number of tracks suitable for biking. They have a brochure, *Mountain Biking Pureora*, which details other riding options. (Despite what this says you certainly can ride on the Waihaha Track.)

### Contacts

**DOC Turangi/Taupo Area Office**: Turanga Pl, Turangi, 07 386 8607
**DOC Pureora Field Centre**: 198 Barryville Rd, Pureora Forest, 07 878 1080
**Turangi Visitor Information Centre**: Ngawaka Pl, Turangi, 07 386 8999, www.laketaupo.co.nz (for history, accommodation and activities)

# Central Plateau

**The Central Plateau is a unique volcanic landscape with stunning and varied scenery and amazing recreational opportunities. From most parts of the North Island this area is readily accessible for a weekend away. From the South Island it is best included in a more lengthy road trip. I suggest you base yourself in Ohakune, National Park or Owhango depending on your après biking interests and style. There is plenty of scope for other recreation around these parts and combining a bike ride or two with some of the country's most spectacular walks will provide action for non-riding members of your group. This region has notoriously bad and, more importantly, very changeable weather, and this must always be considered when venturing into the sticks.**

The 42 Traverse is a classic New Zealand mountain-bike ride and for many people a first foray into wilderness terrain. It is a ride that everyone should do, for its spectacular scenery, ripping downhills and the adventure of point-to-point riding. From a technical point of view it is suitable for most mountain bikers but it's a long one-way ride in remote country so good fitness and some outdoor skills are essential. This is a great ride to do with a large group of people. For smaller groups it is always a good idea to leave a record of your intentions somewhere.

Fishers Track is a little additional something while you are in the area. A sneaky effort-free cruise down this fun four-wheel drive track is just the thing for tired legs after the 42. There is a bit more scenery and plenty of downhill good fun and hooting to be had.

If you are still up for some fine single track after all that and you're heading north then consider riding a trail from the Turangi or Taupo sections of this book, just to completely polish off your legs.

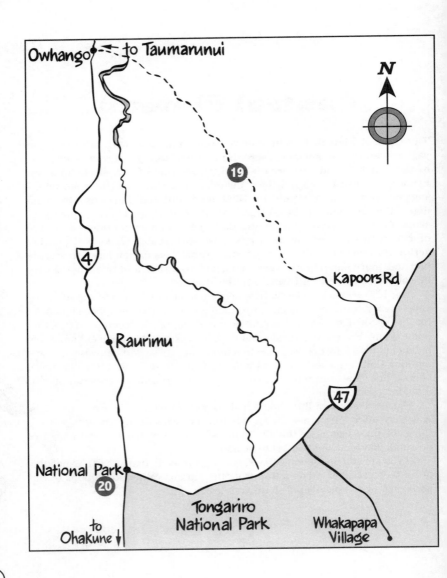

# 42 Traverse

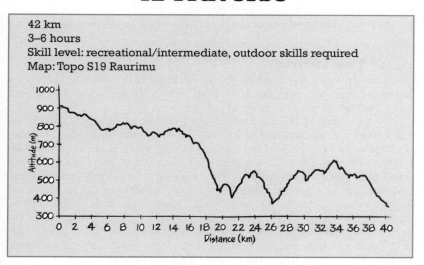

42 km
3–6 hours
Skill level: recreational/intermediate, outdoor skills required
Map: Topo S19 Raurimu

The 42 Traverse or Tongariro Forest Crossing, as it is often called, is an old forest logging road that has pleasantly deteriorated into a four-wheel drive track, excellent for mountain biking. It crosses the Tongariro Forest from east to west between State Highway 47 near Mt Ruapehu and State Highway 4 at Owhango. It is a very popular mountain-bike ride because of the spectacular views, the feeling of isolation and adventure and a very moderate technical challenge, combined with a very satisfying distance.

This ride is suitable for mountain bikers with a reasonable level of fitness and some outdoor skills. It is not very technical riding but the rutted downhills will provide some people with quite a challenge.

The 42 Traverse is named after the original State Forest 42 and, conveniently, is about 42 km long. It's a point-to-point ride, best done with a car shuttle. This gives the ride a distinct downhill bias with an overall drop of about 600m.

Leave a car or get met at the Owhango end of the ride, preferably where the track crosses the Whakapapa River (on Whakapapa Bush Rd). This will mean you don't have to ride the last 2 km gravel uphill back to the main road and will let you finish on a downhill at a picnic area with a decent swimming hole.

Shuttle transport is offered by numerous companies in the area including Howard's Lodge and National Park Backpackers in National Park Village and the Owhango Hotel and Forest Lodge in Owhango, which is convenient.

 ## The riding

The start of the ride is on State Highway 47 at Kapoors Rd, which is 16 km from National Park (on the left) and 33 km from Turangi (on the right). The car park has a DOC information board about the ride.

The first 7 km of the ride descends on gravel before reaching what looks like a work site. You will also find some motorbike jumps here to have a play on. This is the first intersection; turn right (north) and continue on the main track, which you can see heading off over a small rise. The track is marked with yellow-topped posts but these are somewhat erratic. From here the track undulates but mostly descends for about 7 km before reaching the top of the longest descent. Follow the main track, which may well be covered in mountain-bike or motorbike tyre tracks. A couple of short side tracks lead to scenic viewpoints, well worth a look. The views in this section of the ride are probably the best, looking out over the native forest valley and, if the weather is clear enough, back to the three volcanoes of the Central Plateau.

The clay-based downhill gets a little rugged with some decent ruts and rocky sections but is excellent fun. In some parts it appears that chutes have almost been carved out in the track. Speed can get out of hand around here so be careful because it is a long way out if you 'eat it' badly. At about 20 km you will reach the Waione Stream, which you'll sidle along before reaching a crossing point. It is usually ankle-to-calf deep, so it's worth taking your shoes off. I did get wet shorts once when it was at mid-thigh depth and we linked together to cross it, so be careful if it has been raining. There are four smaller stream crossings along the way but most can be ridden through. The climb out of the Waione Stream may require a short walk and then the trail continues to ascend for a couple of kilometres. From here there is some more undulating terrain and the final significant up, a gradual rise of about 7 km, before a similar length downhill to the finish. The terrain changes in the later part of the ride, becoming more bush-like, and the forest floor is a little wetter. There are several short wooden bridges and there's a pretty waterfall. The track officially ends at a DOC sign a short distance before the Whakapapa River crossing. The river bridge is a good place to get picked up. If you are not stopping here it is another 2 km (uphill) back to Owhango where there are pub-style meals, beer and a good-looking new café.

# Fishers Track

> 25 km one way, mostly downhill
> 1.5–3 hours
> Skill level: recreational/intermediate
> Map: Topo S19 Raurimu

By far the nicest way to ride Fishers Track is one way and downhill only. The track starts at about 800 m elevation, rises very briefly and then drops more than 600 vertical metres in its 25 km, with no uphill. It is the perfect ride for the post-42 Traverse day. There is very little pedalling, more stunning scenery and plenty to concentrate your skills on. I wouldn't recommend you ride it in the wet — the clay-based trail gets very slick and it can be a dangerous and frustrating experience.

Several operators in the National Park area will provide shuttle pick-up from the end of Fishers Track. Howard's Lodge has an on-demand service and a regular daily pick-up from the end in the summer, which is great value. If you have your own shuttle driver he or she should head to Raurimu and turn left into Kaitieke Rd, following it to the intersection with Upper Retaruke Rd where the monument is and wait at this point.

## The riding

Fishers Track starts just out of National Park and is an easy ride from the village. Follow Carroll St away from the highway and cross the railway tracks, veering right onto Fishers Rd and following the Fishers Track signpost.

You may see some quaint local signs about security cameras and private property, and may even meet a local character who has been known to try to send people the wrong way. Ignore all this as this track is on public land, and follow the obvious road.

The first 3 or 4 km from National Park is gravel and is slightly uphill. The road soon turns into a four-wheel drive type track and heads into native bush. The next 10 km or so is the crux of Fishers Track. It is downhill all the way and easy to follow — brake-wearing good times. The surface is a combination of clay, rocks (which can be slippery at any time) and some grass.

The track eventually meets a gravel road (Kurua Rd) that continues down the hill and comes out to a three-way intersection near a farmhouse. At this point you turn right onto Upper Retaruke Rd and coast down the gravel near the Retaruke River for about 12 km. At the end of the downhill section of gravel is another intersection and an old monument. This is the pick-up point for the shuttle, so you need not worry about riding out of the depths you have gotten into!

For those crazy enough to even think about riding back to National Park, turn right at this intersection and follow the signs to Raurimu before turning right again at State Highway 4 and continuing the 25 km killer uphill slog.

 **Coffee and food**

If you are based in Ohakune, Utopia Café in Clyde St is a groovy place with excellent food and coffee and is definitely my pick. The Fat Pigeon Garden Café in Tyne St is another option for good food and coffee.

The Powderhorn Chateau is Ohakune's premium accommodation and has two restaurants: the Matterhorn (for fine dining) and the Powderkeg, a popular spot for some après-ride socialising, food and drink. A soak in the Powderhorn's indoor heated pool may be just the ticket for some post-ride relaxation.

If you are staying a little closer to the start in National Park, the Station Café in Findlay St is a great stopping point but does not open until 11am. It has an excellent warm fire on colder days and truckloads of good food. The café has a very entertaining fluoro-jacketed small dog called Max who races the trains that pull in here until they're out of sight. National Park has a lack of cafés open in the morning so bring breakfast or order it from your accommodation and be prepared to ride without a good coffee inside you.

Just up the Whakapapa Rd, the Chateau Tongariro has some feeding options with the upmarket Ruapehu Room restaurant (no jeans or T-shirts allowed) and the Tussock Bar or the casual Pihanga Café and T Bar, which has great food at reasonable prices. The main restaurant does an amazing buffet breakfast but be prepared to pay for the pleasure and don't stuff yourself too full to ride.

At the end of the 42 Traverse the pub in Owhango has classic pub food and environs, and a new café called Out of the Fog has popped up offering more sophisticated surrounds.

##  Accommodation

Both National Park and Ohakune have endless accommodation options and Owhango also has a few offerings. Howard's Lodge in National Park is a good choice with a range of accommodation options and transport for both rides. They also have locked bike storage and a basic workshop with bike stand available for your use, which is very thoughtful.

##  Things to do

Don't get too excited about stopping at the lookout for the famous Raurimu Spiral. Although there is a quirky model of the spiral you are lucky to pick out the real one from the foliage and will only see anything if you happen to time your visit for when a train's passing.

A drive up the Whakapapa or Turoa ski field roads provides some fantastic views on a fine day and during summer Whakapapa runs its chairlift for sightseeing trips and as a starting point for hiking to the Crater Lake.

If you are looking for recreation of the pedestrian kind, the Tongariro Crossing and the Tama Lakes walk in Tongariro National Park stand out. The Tongariro Crossing is New Zealand's most popular one-day walk and is an absolutely stunning trip over some spectacular volcanic geography. The walk does require shuttle transport but this is widely available.

The Tama Lakes walk takes you to the Tama saddle between the mountains Ruapehu and Ngauruhoe (five to six hours return) and has fantastic views and great but refreshing swimming in the lakes. The hike up to the Ruapehu Crater Lake is also a must-do.

The Whakapapa Visitor Centre just past the Chateau has information about these and numerous other walks as well as interesting displays and up-to-date weather information.

The National Park Backpackers has an indoor climbing wall with 55 routes and you can rent all the necessary equipment. They have a range of well-priced accommodation, a spa pool and can provide transport for the 42 Traverse and Fishers Track.

## Contacts

**DOC Whakapapa Visitor Centre**: just past the Chateau, Whakapapa, 07 892 3729

**National Park information**: www.nationalpark.co.nz

**Ruapehu Visitor Information Centre**: 54 Clyde St, Ohakune, 0800 782 734, www.ohakune.info

**Howard's Lodge**: 11–13 Carroll St, National Park, 07 892 2827, www.howardslodge.co.nz

**National Park Backpackers**: Finlay St, National Park, 07 892 2870, www.npbp.co.nz

# Hawke's Bay

**Hawke's Bay is one of those beautiful sunny places that just makes you feel relaxed. The riding is good, the landscape is beautiful and there's plenty of open space. The art deco architecture of Napier is a well-known attraction, and the new development at the wharf area makes it one of the city's happening spots. There are plenty of places for eating, drinking and hanging out around the town. Upmarket Havelock North has many more too and is not far away. Oh, and they have vineyards!**

Hawke's Bay is a little like Taranaki, in that it is not a place you often pass through but a special trip to these parts will guarantee you a great time.

This selection of rides is the majority of what is available in Hawke's Bay, and is plenty to fill up your weekend or long weekend. The Hawke's Bay Mountain Bike Club puts most of its time and effort into developing Eskdale Park and the associated downhill tracks. These are fantastic and suitable for all types of riders and skill levels. The wee trail on Te Mata Peak is more suitable for confident riders as some of it is pretty steep and narrow. Yeoman's Track is a bit of a drive but it is worthwhile if you want a little adventure in a bit more wilderness. It is the kind of ride that most riders can enjoy, with few technical challenges and a great chance to get out into the Ruahine foothills.

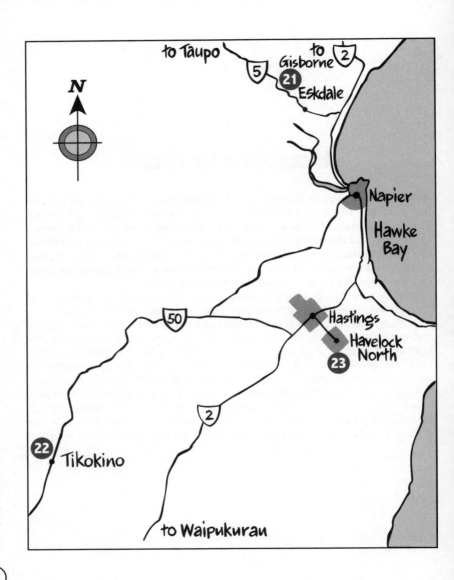

# Eskdale Mountain Bike Park

More than 50 km of marked single track
1–2 days
Skill level: all
Map: Hawke's Bay Mountain Bike Club map

Eskdale Mountain Bike Park is a great place and the Hawke's Bay Mountain Bike Club is doing a fantastic job here. The Pan Pac-owned exotic forest is riddled with well thought-out and built single track with trails suitable for all levels of ability. The trails are well marked, link up and easily provide a good weekend of riding alone.

Hawke's Bay has a great climate for mountain-bike riding with a lot of sunshine and not too much rain. In summer the trails at Eskdale are generally very hard-packed with a sprinkling of pine needles. There is next to no undergrowth in the forest so the trails stay clear and the shade of the big trees keeps things a little bit cooler out of the sun.

 **The riding**

Eskdale is 19 km north-west of Napier on State Highway 5 (Napier–Taupo Rd). The park is signposted at Waipunga Rd on the right just past Eskdale Village.

You need a permit to ride in Eskdale. You can either join the Hawke's Bay Mountain Bike Club (www.hawkesbaymtb.co.nz) for a year or buy a $5 three-week permit from any bike shop in the area, the visitor information office in Napier or Bayview Four Square or Whitebay World of Lavender Café in Eskdale. You also get an amazing and very accurate waterproof map with some suggested riding loops. It's a bargain.

At least 50 km of trails are clearly marked with proper signs and are accurately represented on the map. Most are two-way but the preferred riding direction is marked on the map. They are also graded for difficulty and this is marked on the signs. There are also other trails being built, some existing trails that don't have names and plenty more forestry and four-wheel drive tracks.

Remember that this is a working forest and you must obey all warnings about forestry operations and out-of-bounds areas.

More recently the free-ride and downhill side of things has been developed with some wild-looking structures starting to appear in the forest and some fast and technical trails for those truly looking for this type of riding. These trails are all marked on the map with a double black diamond.

# Yeoman's Track

17 km loop or 15 km out-and-back on the track
2–4 hours
Skill level: recreational
Map: Topo U21 Kereru and U22 Ongaonga

Yeoman's Track is in the Ruahine Forest Park 100 km south-west of Napier. The trail is the remains of an old logging track that the regenerating forest has encroached on, now making it a combination of easily rideable benched single and double track. The track is essentially non-technical but has a few slippery sections where slick clay and damp rocks can make things exciting. It is suitable for all keen riders with some outdoor skills.

Interesting stands along the track provide botanical information and tell the milling history of the area, including the story of Yeoman's Mill, which operated here from the 1920s to 1950s.

There are several options for riding the track: you can make a 17 km loop by riding gravel logging roads to the northern end of the track via Ellis Hut and then riding though it, as described here; or you can ride in from the southern end of the track to the northern end and Ellis Hut and then back again, staying in the bush the whole way.

 **The riding**

To get to Yeoman's Track from Napier follow State Highway 50 south-west. At 70 km from Napier and 3 km past Tikokino, turn right into Makaroro Rd and

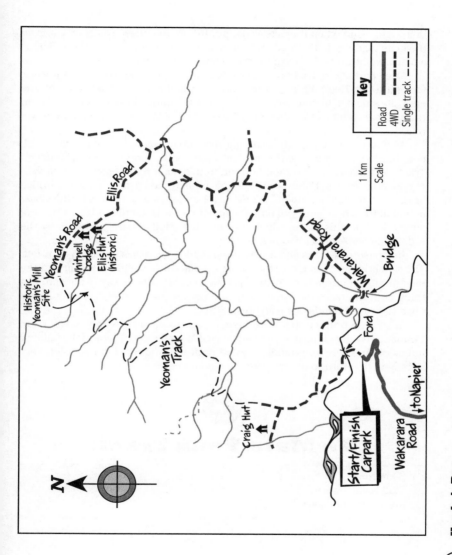

Key

Road
4WD
Single track

1 Km
Scale

N

Historic Yeoman's Mill Site

Whitwell Lodge

Yeoman's Road

Ellis Road

Ellis Hut (historic)

Yeoman's Track

Craig Hut

Start/Finish Carpark

Wakarara Road

Bridge

Ford

Wakarara Road ↓ to Napier

Hawke's Bay

83

then right again when it meets Wakarara Rd. Follow these roads 28 km from the main highway to the road end where a ford crosses the river. Here there is a map and information board for the Ruahine Forest Park.

After parking, don't bother putting your shoes on as you ford the river straight away. Head directly across the river and find the gravel road on the opposite side just to your left of the high bank. Follow this section of old road (a small part is almost washed out) for less than a kilometre to a major gravel road.

At this point, if you are planning the out-and-back trip along the track continue straight (left) and you will find a sign for the southern end of Yeoman's Track. For the loop, turn right here on to this main road through the private commercial forest. Follow this section initially down and across a bridge before climbing, to a total of 7.8 km, then turn left at a sign for Ellis Rd. Coast downhill from here until you pass the historic Ellis Hut, built in 1884. Stop and have a look at this place, which has an interesting history, and pass by the rather unloved-looking Withnell Lodge.

Just past these huts and a rise in the road is Yeoman's Track on your left. The sign is about 50 m inside the grassy double track. Continue riding past the old mill site and from here the trail is easy to follow all the way to the end. The track is in the trees the whole way and passes through regenerating native bush as well as stands of eucalyptus.

At the end of the trail you will come out to a clearing with a gravel road. Continue straight along the road and you will complete your loop at the familiar intersection where you initially turned right into the main gravel road. Veer right here to return to the river ford and your car.

# Te Mata Peak Track

5 km loop
Skill level: intermediate
Map: board at start

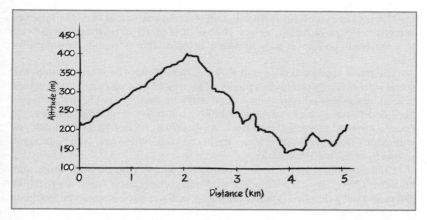

The stunning Te Mata Peak near Havelock North is well worth a visit for its beauty, sensational views over the countryside and mountain-bike track. The peak is a publicly accessible park that was gifted to the people of Hawke's Bay and is administered by a trust. There are many kilometres of pristine walking tracks that are not available to mountain bikes, but fortunately there is one very short but very sweet mountain-bike specific track.

The track is fun and fast, not for the whole family and definitely not a big day out. I could happily have done it several more times and you definitely get some good exercise riding up. It's well worth it.

## The riding

Te Mata Peak is 4.5 km from Havelock North, a good place to start your day with its fine selection of cafés. From the town centre, follow the Te Mata Rd, turning right at the second roundabout into Simla Ave and continuing on to Te Mata Peak Rd, following the clear signs to Te Mata Peak. Park at the first car park, just through the main gates on your right. There is a map board here that shows the mountain-bike track. The Te Mata Peak brochure you can get from the Napier visitor centre doesn't have this trail marked on it.

From the car park ride the 2.5 km uphill to the summit. On the way up you will see the clearly marked mountain-bike track on your right on a left-hand hairpin corner just before the top. It is well worth going right to the summit for a look.

The trail is essentially downhill, and steep in parts. It is very hard-packed and either jumpy or humpy as you choose. It is pretty narrow and on the side of a steep hill so take it easy first-time around. This is seat-down riding for sure.

The track zigzags, bumps and sidles its way down; there are a number of spots with several options and plenty of jumps. After a bit of an uphill, which is hard on the legs with the seat so low, and a bit more downhill that ends in a big jump (with a chicken-line, thankfully) the track stops and you need to cross a lowered fence and turn right. After a short section of single track you will meet Chambers Walk, a wider multi-use trail, where you turn right again to return to the main car park.

Credit definitely needs to be given to the people who built the mountain-bike track here. They have made a wild-ride roller-coaster track for real bike riders and not a dumbed-down version of a walking track suitable for grandma on her 10-speed.

 **Coffee and food**

For good coffee and breakfast try Provedore Restaurant (60 West Quay, Ahuriri) in Napier's wharf area. It is a café by day and a wine bar and bistro at night. In the centre of Napier, the Bohemian-style Ujazi (28 Tennyson St) has good, sizeable food and loud music. Café DMP (80 Dickens St) has an award-winning barista, good brekkie and lunch and is open for early-morning starts.

For a good evening meal, the West Quay area is a popular choice with restaurants such as the Gintrap and Thirsty Whale serving solid and tasty meals with outdoor seating among the port atmosphere.

Havelock North has a number of café choices, but the shocking pink Pipi's (16 Joll Rd) is a great pick for afternoon or evening wood-fired pizzas.

Of course the Hawke's Bay region is well known for vineyard and winery restaurants, most of which specialise in lunch and some in dinner. Te Awa Winery (2375 State Highway 50, Hastings) is one of the better relaxed ones. Black Barn (Black Barn Rd, Havelock North) comes recommended and the classic Mission Estate (198 Church Rd, Greenmeadows, Napier) always gets good reviews.

 **Accommodation**

Napier and the surrounding area has a lot of accommodation with every option from luxury lodges and cottages to backpackers and plenty of dodgy motels. Try the Westshore area for decent motels that are walking distance to beach.

There are the standard inner-city camping options, which are always hard to recommend — it may be nicer to put up a tent near the start of Yeoman's Track.

**Things to do**

With Hawke's Bay's reputation for fantastic hot weather, you may be looking for a swimming spot. Westshore Beach just north of the city is the main local choice. It is stony and quite steep but reasonably safe. Don't swim at Marine Parade as it is notoriously unsafe and there have been many drownings caused by huge rogue waves. Further out of town the choices are better. Forty minutes north, Waipatiki is a good spot and, 40 minutes south, Waimarama and Ocean Beach are generally where it is at.

If you are riding Yeoman's Track, the Ruahine Ranges are loaded with great tramping opportunities for those with a pedestrian bent.

Napier is renowned for its art deco architecture, and taking a self-guided or guided trip is educational and fascinating if you're interested in that kind of thing.

As everyone with an interest in wine will know, Hawke's Bay is also ripe with vineyards and wineries. There are many opportunities for tasting and visiting, with or without dining. The visitor information centre has plenty of information about the wine scene or you could also try www.hawkesbaywines.com.

---

**Contacts**

**Hawke's Bay Mountain Bike Club**: www.hawkesbaymtb.co.nz
**Napier Visitor Information Centre**: 100 Marine Parade, Napier, 06 834 1911, www.hawkesbaynz.com

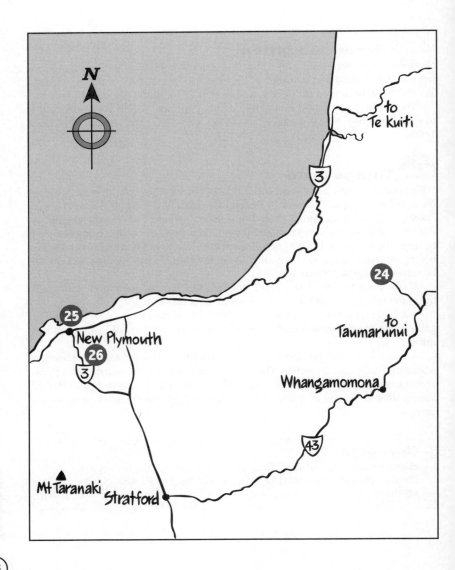

# Taranaki

If you haven't been to Taranaki recently — or ever — it is time to go. New Plymouth is not the kind of place you pass through, so a special trip is generally required. There are plenty of reasons to make the trip. Firstly, New Plymouth is cool, with an amazing location on the sea and right under the nose of a spectacular mountain. It has a sophisticated cultural scene with a very high café to population ratio, and recreation and relaxation opportunities abound. That is without even considering the mountain biking.

The mountain biking in this weekend chapter consists of the epic Moki–Rerekapa Loop, which is a big day out for experienced and adventurous riders, and two smaller and much less testing rides close to New Plymouth — the Coastal Walkway, Huatoki and Te Henui walkways and the Lake Mangamahoe Forest trails.

Depending on where you are travelling from, a long weekend (or more) in Taranaki is a good idea. It would allow time for the big ride (if that suits you), then a leisurely sightseeing and coffee-stop ride around the town trails while recovering the next day. This could perhaps be followed by an afternoon of cultural activity or a trip up the mountain, and then a fun ride in the local forest trails the following day.

# Moki–Rerekapa Loop

44 km loop
5–8 hours
Skill level: intermediate, outdoor skills required
Map: Topo R19 Whangamomona and R18 Ohura

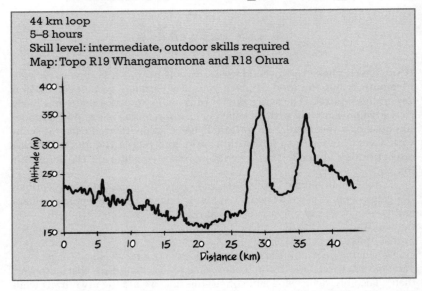

Previously known as the 'Mythical Moki', this loop ride in the wilds of Taranaki is a big adventure. The loop incorporates the moderately technical and wilderness single track of the Moki and Rerekapa tracks, the double track of the Moki Rd and a 12 km gravel road section between them.

Although the track is easy enough to follow once you get to it, it is fairly remote, rugged in parts, and likely to have some debris on it. There will be some pushing required. You'll need to be keen for an epic day, and you'll need some wilderness experience. In the wet, the mud of the farm road is a sticky nightmare and the overgrowth on the track will keep you drenched for most of the ride, so it is not recommended. This is definitely the kind of ride to start early — and take plenty of food and water.

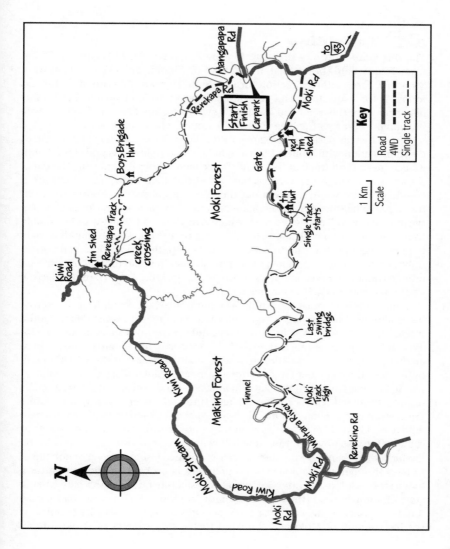

**N**

**Key**
Road
4WD
Single track

Scale
1 Km

Start/Finish Carpark

Nangapapa Rd
Kerekapa Rd
Moki Rd
to 43
Gate
red tin shed
tin hut
Single track starts
Boys Brigade Hut
Kerekapa Track
tin shed
creek crossing
Kiwi Road
Moki Forest
Makino Forest
Kiwi Road
Moki Stream
Kiwi Road
Moki Rd
Last swing bridge
Tunnel
Moki Track Sign
Waitara River
Moki Rd
Moki Rd
Rerekino Rd

Taranaki

**The riding**

The ride starts off State Highway 43 (The Forgotten World Highway), 73 km from Taumarunui (be warned, this is a lot of winding gravel), or 89 km from Stratford. From either direction turn off State Highway 43 onto Moki Rd and follow it for 8 km, then take a right-hand turn into Mangapapa Rd. A short distance down this road and just past a sign for campervans and toilets there is a camping area with tables and an old mining relic — park here.

From the car park on Mangapapa Rd ride back the way you have come to the intersection with Moki Rd. Turn right here and follow this gravel road until it becomes a farm track at the 'Moki Track' sign. About 3.5 km from the car is a gate with a white marker just past a red tin shed. From here there are a couple of other white markers but they are not consistent. Follow the farm track. At 5.5 km there is another gate with no obvious marker. Continue along the main track well above the river, which is to your right. This silty-clay double track rolls along the hillside before coming to a short, steep climb that may require a bike push to the top. Just after the top, the track forks and you go right down a steep and slippery downhill and soon come to a tin hut with an orange triangle marker and a step stile to the left (6.7 km). Here the narrow single track starts and the fun begins.

The track is obvious the whole way but unmarked. Small ferns overgrow the track, there are some rutted creeks and there may be some debris on the track. The narrow track is in native bush and scrub and at times it can be a bit slow. It feels quite remote and it would be a surprise to see anyone else. There are five swing bridges and a dozen or so wooden bridges that show DOC's commitment to the track but I'm not sure how much regular work they do on it.

At 14.4 km you reach the last and longest swing bridge and the trail opens up into farmland. Cross the bridge and turn right over a gently undulating grassy trail with a couple of muddy bogs. At about 17 km you will reach a gate with a 'Moki Track' sign for traffic in the opposite direction. At this point veer right on the less obvious track that follows the river — don't go up the hill on the farm road. Another kilometre later you come to a short but very cool tunnel to pass through and somewhere around here is probably a good place for a lunch stop. A kilometre after the tunnel is a concrete bridge with a gate and the start of a gravel road (the continuation of Moki Rd). Follow this road for 2.5 km, being wary of the cattle, or more specifically some rather large bulls. At the intersection of Moki and Rerekino roads, stay straight on Moki Rd and follow it until it veers right onto Kiwi Rd.

Kiwi Rd is mostly gravel but the significant climb and descent is actually sealed, which is most appreciated at this stage of the day! A couple of kilometres after the bottom of the big hill at 34.5 km the Rerekapa Track is clearly marked on the right just before a tin shed.

Large orange blazes lead across the farmland and you have to cross a small creek before heading uphill on a cow-bogged track on the left side of the valley. Soon this track turns into single track and is easy to follow. There may be a few small obstacles but generally this track is wider and clearer than the Moki section, although it is definitely more slippery when wet. The track climbs then sidles around the hill before reaching a saddle. Some of the nicest single track leads down to the Boys' Brigade hut and track signpost.

From this point it is mostly downhill on a grassy single track until you reach farmland. The track remains obvious the whole time. You will pass a DOC workers' hut before coming out on Mangapapa Rd shortly after. Turn right here and it is only 400 m back to the car.

# New Plymouth Foreshore

20 km
1–2 hours
Skill level: recreational
Map: New Plymouth free street guide and walkways guides

This is a great way to get a scenic view of New Plymouth. No technical riding here, but a beautiful cruise along the dramatic Coastal Walkway and the easy single track of the Huatoki and Te Henui walkways (open to bikes). Being realistic, if you have ridden the Moki the day before you probably need an easy day with plenty of opportunity for coffee stops.

 **The riding**

Start by getting a map at New Plymouth's Puke Ariki complex, which houses

Taranaki

the museum and information centre. The New Plymouth district free street guide is probably the best as the fold-out map covers the whole city, but they also have more detailed guides to the Huatoki and Te Henui walkways, which have interesting historical information. There are any number of ways you could ride these trails and below is just one route that seemed to flow well.

After you have checked out the stunning new museum and had a quick café stop, head away from the sea to the start of the Huatoki Walkway on Courtenay St just down the hill from the end of Carrington St. You will pass through a car park and under a viaduct before the real track starts. The trail is easy to follow with good signs, and is a lovely easy single track through the bushy stream valley. There are a couple of road crossings and it is probably best to pop out of the trail at Camden St to head over to the Te Henui Track. This is done by turning left out of Camden St onto Huatoki St, right into Carrington St at a small cluster of shops, left into Tarahua Rd, right into Junction St and left into Durham Ave where the Te Henui Track starts.

The Te Henui Track is similarly lush, easy stream-valley trail riding. From where you enter the track it is straightforward all the way to the coast about 4 km away. Just before the coast you will go under the viaduct of Devon St East. If you climb the stairs here and head left on Devon St East the Zanziba Café will make a good stop. You can continue following this street east until it becomes Clemow Rd and heads to Lake Rotomanu near the Waiwhakaiho River mouth. Follow your nose to the coast and pick up the start of the Coastal Walkway, which you can follow for 7 km all the way to New Plymouth's port. This paved and stylishly designed multi-use path is beautiful. In summer flowering pohutukawa, crashing waves, parks and coastal planting make it something all cities should be envious of. From the port, retrace your pedal strokes back to Puke Ariki.

# Lake Mangamahoe Forest

Up to 20 km
1–2.5 hours
Skill level: all
Map: from visitor centre and on board at trail head

The Lake Mangamahoe Forest is New Plymouth's main mountain-bike specific trail area and is free to use. As with most areas like this, the trails are constantly evolving as the local mountain-bike club and individuals put in the huge amount of hard work to keep things developing and interesting. A basic mountain-bike trail and walking map is available from the information centre at Puke Ariki, and there is also a map board at the start of the tracks. These two do seem to be different, and the map board is probably more accurate.

In early 2007 the trails in this area were in good condition, not overgrown and consisted of fun exotic-forest single track with some seriously big downhill tracks definitely not to be ridden unintentionally!

There is some signage, mostly marking the downhill trails, but the majority of tracks are not marked. To ride here for a couple of hours you will likely re-ride some things numerous times trying to cover all the tracks but it is all good fun and sweet single track.

 ## The riding

The Lake Mangamahoe Forest is 10 km south of New Plymouth on State Highway 3. The lake and main recreation area has a separate entrance at the 'Mangamahoe Forest' sign. There are toilets, picnic tables and walking trails here. For the mountain-biking tracks turn left at Plantation Rd just after this area, then veer left and park shortly afterwards just outside a metal gate that has a map board.

It's hard to get really lost here. The forest is a relatively small area and is edged in by a river to your right (east) when facing away from the main road and the lake to your left (west). The main ridge of the forest runs essentially north–south between these two. The main forestry road (Mangamahoe Rd) is between the trails and the lake and you can usually come out on to this at some point if you wish.

Probably the best way to get orientated and started here is to head straight up the gravel road and turn right on to the Highlands Track, which will take you to the middle of the main ridge. From here you can turn left and follow the zigzag track as it weaves across the ridge or turn right along the ridge and eventually head left off the ridge following one of the non-black trails and continuing in an anticlockwise loop. A note of caution here: some of the black trails are steep and technical but good fun for skilled riders and others have some big drops, gaps and jumps that are certainly not for most people. If you are tempted, some scouting is probably a good idea. Look out for Jump Run, Rugged, #1 DH and the Line, all marked with triple black crosses.

It is always difficult to provide a specific guide to mountain-bike park areas, especially when they are constantly evolving and not particularly well mapped or signed. However, the important thing to know is that the trails here are obvious, maintained, have some good points of reference and are in a confined area where you can't go too far wrong. All in all, it's a great place for a scoot around, especially if you are still recovering from the Moki!

You can find a Mangamahoe mountain-bike track map on the council website www.newplymouthnz.com by searching under 'Mangamahoe'.

##  Coffee and food

New Plymouth has plenty of good options for food and drink with a seeming abundance of excellent cafés. Devon St both east and west in the centre of town is a good place to start, and you won't have to look far to find something to your taste. You could try Mookai, which has good food, coffee and music, the Empire, with good food and a sweet courtyard, the cool Ultra Lounge café and bar, with a great deck, or Chaos, with nice-looking deli-style food. There are also cafés at both the Govett-Brewster Art Gallery and Puke Ariki. If you happen to be in Inglewood (or can make the diversion), Macfarlanes Caffe is an original coffee roaster in the district. It has excellent coffee and sensational fruit tarts, among other things.

##  Accommodation

New Plymouth has all types of accommodation, and information on this can be found on the internet, in guidebooks such as *Lonely Planet* or from the visitor centre at Puke Ariki. Many of the motels are on the main roads into town. If you are looking to camp, the old-style seaside camping ground right on Fitzroy Beach is a winner. There is free camping at the suggested parking spot for the Moki, with no facilities.

**Things to do**

An obvious opportunity for sightseeing in Taranaki is the mountain itself. There is plenty of opportunity for tramping and walking with more than 180 km of tracks on the mountain — visit a DOC office for up-to-date track information and advice. These are located at North Egmont visitor information centre, Dawson Falls visitor information centre or the Stratford DOC office. North Egmont is the closest route up the mountain from town and a great place for a scenic drive and view, weather permitting.

If you don't ride the Coastal Walkway then a walk along this stunning foreshore is a must.

Things to do opportunities abound in Taranaki. The area has a particularly strong surfing reputation and there are plenty of beaches. Heading south-west around the coast Oakura and Opunake have particularly well-rated surf spots and Back Beach just near the port is a good option close to town. Fitzroy Beach is a nice swimming spot, as closer to town waves crash on to the boulder bank. There is also an impressive outdoor pool at Kawaroa towards the port end of the waterfront.

New Plymouth has a surprisingly healthy arts and culture scene. The Govett-Brewster is a contemporary art gallery with an impressive New Zealand-wide reputation. It houses a permanent collection of the work of kinetic artist and film-maker Len Lye, who is also responsible for the *Wind Wand* sculpture on the waterfront. Anyone with an interest in modern and contemporary art would be foolish to miss this gallery and its excellent shop.

Puke Ariki in the centre of town on the waterfront is the city's new museum, library and information centre and is a spectacular complex. The museum has a strong interactive focus and is a fun way to find out about the history and geography of the area. You could spend hours in here or use it as a quick stop and a chance to gather some local information and maps or check out the café before a ride through the walkways.

## Contacts

**New Plymouth Visitor Centre**: Puke Ariki, Ariki St, 06 759 6060, www.taranaki.co.nz

**Taranaki**

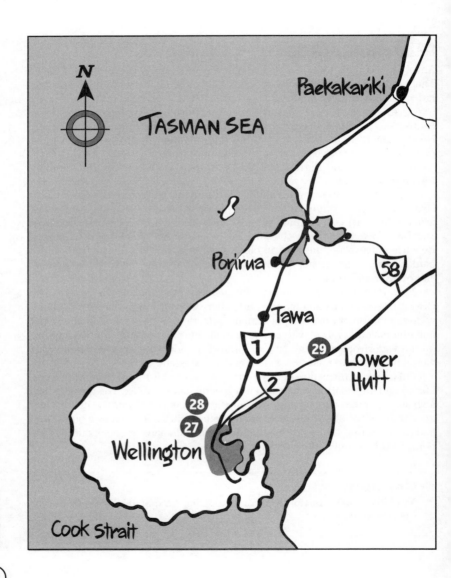

# Wellington

**Wellington is New Zealand's most impressive mountain-biking city. It is a proactive bike-friendly place that encourages trail riding in a number of inner-city areas. It has a collection of green-belt trails that allow commuters to ride off-road to work and head out for a central-city skid at lunch time. Wellington also has some sensational purpose-built trails close to the city, regional parks that support riding and plenty of tracks a little further afield.**

Wellington is home to the legendary authors the Kennett Brothers, the Vorb cycling website and *Spoke* magazine as well as numerous other passionate mountain bikers who all keep things rolling on the mountain-biking front.

There is plenty of biking to do in Wellington and a weekend is not enough time to cover that much of it. But, in the spirit of the best long weekend away, this selection will give you a jolly good taste of what's on offer. Makara Peak is an awesome collection of purpose-built mountain-bike trails, with a variety of levels to suit all riders. The rideable Skyline Walkway is a big day out that embraces numerous trails. It has plenty of great trail riding, amazing views and a special kind of epic ride satisfaction. For something a little different the Belmont Trig ride lets you see the city from a different angle on a fun single track.

# 27

# Makara Peak

> More than 25 km of single track
> Up to 4 hours
> Skill level: all
> Map: Makara Peak Mountain Bike Park map

The Makara Peak Mountain Bike Park is Wellington's jewel of purpose-built trails. It has been a designated mountain-biking area for almost 10 years and local mountain bikers have done a superb job of building more than 25 km of single track.

The peak itself is just over 400 m high and about 260 m above the car park. This provides for perfect-gradient uphills, long and flowing downhills and enough steep bits for some pretty sweet descents. The hillside is a mix of regenerating native bush on the southern side and some gorse and pest plants up top in the open. There are natural rock and root obstacles and there's an increasing number of man-made structures to provide stability and enhance the flow of the tracks as well as provide technical challenges.

 **The riding**

To get to Makara Peak Mountain Bike Park make your way to the suburb of Karori and head along Karori Rd until you see South Karori Rd on your left. Makara is signposted from here, and the car park is about 1 km along on your right. There are toilets and water at the park.

It is a good idea to have a map of the mountain-bike tracks and the easiest thing is to print one from www.makarapeak.org.nz. You can also get maps from Mud Cycles on Karori Rd.

There are any number of trail combinations you could ride at Makara, but a good start is to ride a classic loop such as this: head up the lovely winding Koru track, which is an easy uphill, continue over on to Sally Alley and keep gradually heading up on Missing Link and Aratihi. This combination is now fine single track all the way to the top of Makara Peak and is a simply lovely way to gain a heap of elevation. From the top of Makara, heading down via Ridgeline, Ridgeline extension, SWIGG and Starfish is great fun for riders with reasonable intermediate-level skills.

Good descriptions of the individual tracks are on the Makara website but in general the easy tracks or those suitable for beginners are Koru, Magic Carpet, Lazy Fern, Sally Alley and the four-wheel drive tracks. For intermediate riders add on Livewires, Snake Charmer, Missing Link, Aratihi, Zac's, Varley's, SWIGG, Starfish and Leaping Lizard. For downhill-style and more advanced technical riders there's Ridgeline, Vertigo and Trickle Falls but bear in mind that these last two are extreme downhill-style riding tracks.

On the other side of the valley from Makara Peak is Wright's Hill. It has an uphill track known as Salvation (part of the Skyline Walkway) and a downhill track known as Deliverance. Salvation has a perfect uphill gradient and is a tree-clad, winding 3 km. It is non-technical and suitable for all riders. It is also bi-directional and multi-use. For skilled riders Deliverance is sensational and is my favourite Wellington track hands-down. It is a technical rocky single track that heads down into a damp native bush valley over a couple of kilometres. With a lot of challenges and never a dull moment you could do this track many times without getting tired of it. These two tracks link up at both the top and bottom. To find these tracks from the Makara car park, turn right on to South Karori Rd then left onto Hazelwood Ave followed by a right into Fitzgerald Pl. At the end of this street you will see the Skyline Track to Wright's Hill (Salvation) signposted.

# Skyline Walkway (Mt Kaukau to Red Rocks)

32 km
4–8 hours or split over two days
Skill level: intermediate
Map: Explore Wellington Skyline Track (basic map to Makara)

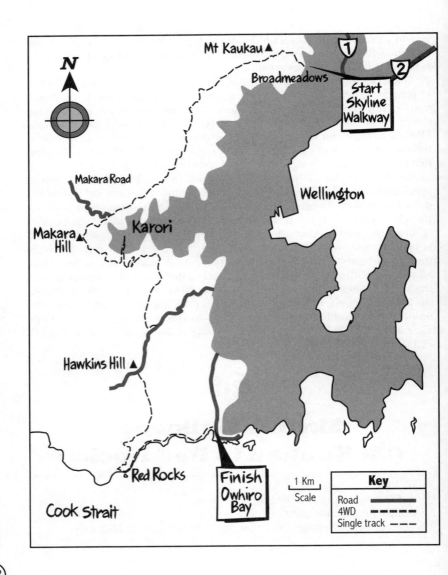

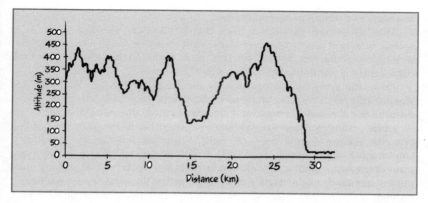

The Skyline Walkway is a great mountain-biking traverse of Wellington's outer green belt. It provides a fantastic perspective on Wellington from the hills above the city and great views in all directions. The track is a combination of open single and double track over farmland, sweet single track including some of Makara Peak's best trails and the legendary Hawkins Hill to Red Rocks track.

The complete ride is a big day out and requires good fitness and endurance, especially because of the amount of uphill. The riding is not particularly technical apart from some sections towards the end of the Red Rocks Track that can always be walked. Overall the track is a fun ride, incorporating some classic Wellington mountain biking. It is challenging for its distance and hills and a very satisfying little adventure close to the city. Be warned that this is a ride to be careful on when it is windy!

 ## The riding

To ride from the Mt Kaukau start of the track, you need to find the entrance off Sirsi Tce in Broadmeadows. By far the easiest way to do this is with a Wellington street map as the maze of streets in this area can be very confusing. The starting point is marked with a Wellington City Council sign, and the gradient looks intimidating! Head up the sealed path and take the first narrow dirt single track on your left just as the climb flattens. If you come to a water reservoir you have gone too far. From here the route to the top of Mt Kaukau is obvious and marked by lollipop-shaped blazes.

The 360-degree panorama from the Mt Kaukau viewing platform is spectacular, and is just the start in the ever-changing perspective of greater Wellington on this ride. In fact, you can see so far afield that you can spot both coasts and the South Island on a clear day.

From the viewing platform follow the signs for Skyline Walkway and Makara Hill Rd. There are numerous exits from the track into most of the suburbs that it passes through, and sometimes these disembarking tracks can be a little confusing. However, keeping a close eye on the markers and heading towards Makara should see you right. From Mt Kaukau the track is a combination of fun double track and narrow farmland single track. There are some short steep uphills and rugged downhill sections. Overall it is pretty good fun for farmland. As the track nears the suburb of Karori it becomes a tighter formed single track and heads through foliage (including a wee bit of gorse). The next section is in a lovely piece of pine forest and is one of the sweetest pieces of trail in the ride. Shortly after this the track pops out onto Makara Rd at 10.5 km from the start.

From Makara Rd the track heads up and over Makara Peak and takes in some of the best trails in the mountain-bike park. Where the track meets the sealed road, cross over and head right then immediately left into the single track, which heads fairly obviously uphill. At this point the track is not marked by name but it's called Varley's Track and is marked on all the maps of the Makara Peak Mountain Bike Park. This is a nice gradient, switchbacked track that takes you three-quarters of the way to the top of Makara Peak. When you reach the end of the track at a gravel road, cross over and head straight into Zac's Track, which will take you just about to the Makara summit. Up here there is a map board of the mountain-bike park and signs for some of the world's more interesting riding destinations.

You can head down to the Makara car park any way you like, but if you are not familiar with the area the most popular choice would probably be via Ridgeline, Ridgeline extension, SWIGG and Starfish. These are all shown on the map board and link together right down to the bottom of the hill. This is a very fine combination of challenging technical downhill in the open and flowing lush bush-clad trail. All very nice.

The mountain-bike car park at Makara is a good stop for water and to use the plushest toilets that you'll see. This is about the 15 km point and near enough to halfway. If you are planning to do the complete ride over two days then this is a good place to press pause. To really make the most of the local mountain biking, you could continue on and ride up Salvation on Wright's Hill and duck back down Deliverance (the lushest trail in Wellington). It would be rude not to ride it at some point, and is a perfect way to top off the first half of the Skyline Walkway (although Deliverance is not officially part of the track).

A short detour left down South Karori Rd will take you to a well-stocked dairy if you need a food stop. If you are in need of a bike shop then you can find Mud Cycles a little further along Karori Rd.

If you are heading on towards Red Rocks, turn right onto South Karori Rd from the car park and then left onto Hazelwood Ave followed by a right into Fitzgerald Place. At the end of this street is the uphill track to the top of Wright's Hill. The track is signposted here as the Skyline Track to Wright's Hill but is known locally as 'Salvation'. It is a superb example of uphill riding pleasure, with 3 km of bush-covered, perfect-gradient uphill switchbacks to the car park below the Wright's Hill summit.

From the car park head right on the sealed road before taking the first right on to gravel only about 100 m later. Turn right again at a gravel intersection less than a kilometre further on. This part of the track is not very well signposted but the main track is clear. You may or may not be able to see a sign for Hawkins Hill and the Roller Coaster, which is where you are heading. When the gravel track meets the Sanctuary Fence Line Track around the Karori Sanctuary (it is pretty obvious), turn right. The wind turbine of Hawkins Hill looks tantalisingly close but unfortunately a very nasty climb separates you from it.

The double-track Sanctuary Fence Line Track is the nastiest piece of the whole ride, mostly due to an evil section of uphill known locally as 'the grovel'. Suffer through this climb then, as the track flattens out and the fence curves clearly to the left, you will see a hole in the small fence on your right between two posts. Jump through this gap and head right on the sealed road leading away from the wind turbine and towards the golf ball-shaped radar station.

Follow this road as it climbs for 1.5 km until you reach the castle on your right. Just past this on your left are several signs including one to Pariwhero (Red Rocks). From here you can clearly see the Red Rocks Track on the ridge and it looks rather spectacular. Several hundred metres down the hill on your right the Red Rocks Track is signposted and turns off. Don't miss this. The track that goes straight down from this intersection is the Tip Track, a steep uphill and downhill track to Happy Valley.

After a further 1 km there is another intersection, with the Red Rocks Track marked to the right. From here the track is rocky and steep with only a couple of very short uphill sections. The sometimes very loose surface is sketchy and can be dangerous so don't get carried away with speed. The views of Cook Strait and the South Island are spectacular and the drop to the left off the narrow ridge sections is similarly awesome.

The last couple of hundred metres have a loose and rocky surface and are deeply rutted. This is a challenging section to ride, good fun if you are able, but better walked if you are in any doubt.

When the track meets the sea you have reached Red Rocks. Turn left and follow the beachy road to Owhiro Bay for 3.5 km. From here, make your way back to town via Happy Valley Rd, get picked up or call a cab!

# Belmont Trig

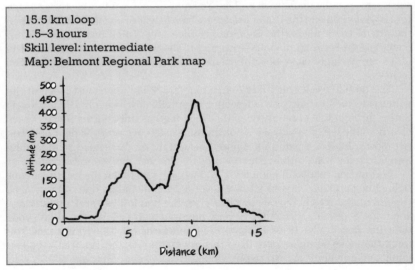

15.5 km loop
1.5–3 hours
Skill level: intermediate
Map: Belmont Regional Park map

For something a little different in Wellington, the Belmont Regional Park has some fun mountain-biking tracks and a bunch of other recreational opportunities. The Belmont Trig ride takes you over the high point of the park, challenging your fitness and providing sensational views in all directions, and then heads into the best of the park's sweet single track and a lush stream valley.

 **The riding**

To complete this ride as a loop the best place to park is at the Cornish St entrance to the regional park. To find this, head towards Petone on State Highway 2 and turn left just under the Petone overpass into Cornish St. Park at the end of this short industrial street and you will see the end of the track and the sign for the Korokoro Dam.

From this parking spot, ride out of Cornish St and turn left on to the main road (State Highway 2). Ride along here for 2.5 km, being super careful about traffic on this busy road. Turn left into Dowse Dr and follow this uphill before turning left into Stratton St at 5.5 km and following the signs for Belmont Regional Park. Just after entering the park, the first track on your left leads to Belmont Trig and is signposted.

The ride up to the trig point is a bit of a harsh one, a no-nonsense 3.5 km grind. Initially the track is very steep and follows a dirt farm road but the gradient eases off, making the majority of the track pleasantly rideable. Across the farmland the track is completely exposed and if the sun is out it is a hot and sweaty climb. The trig is at about a 450 m altitude and, having come right up from sea level at your car 11 km away, this is a decent effort. From the top the views are definitely worth it, especially on a clear and sunny day. The 360-degree panorama takes in the whole of Wellington Harbour, the city, the west coast, the Hutt Valley and the South Island.

After spending some time admiring the view, cooling off (or sheltering from the wind if it's one of those days) and having a snack, turn and face the harbour mouth and head away from the trig on this single track. This is the Puke Ariki Track, and part of the continuous traverse of the park.

The track is initially a combination of open clay and regenerating scrub and native bush. It is all single track from here on down, not too technical but jolly good fun with flowing corners, steep sections and obstacles. As the track gets closer to the stream, the bush becomes thicker and older and the air cooler. Eventually the track meets the Korokoro Stream and from here it follows the river valley out.

The track mostly undulates gently beside the stream, but also zigzags across it with numerous rideable crossings. It is fun and beautiful single track in a quiet valley that feels miles from anywhere.

At a little more than 14 km you will come to a T intersection where you turn right to follow the river down the valley. From here there are a lot of well-made bridges and a narrow gravelled trail, where you may well meet walkers. About a kilometre later you will sadly re-enter the industrial world and be reunited with your car.

You can print off a map of the Belmont Regional Park from the website — search for 'Belmont map' or get one from the park.

 **Coffee and food**

Wellington is a haven of excellent cafés and in a weekend you surely won't be able to try them all. It may be important to get a good coffee or breakfast on the way to Makara and, if so, the Kelburn Village is the place to stop. Mode is a great choice for coffee and food but there are several others that do a very fine job too. Once you get to Karori the cafés thin out and your best shot is the upmarket Arobake bakery at the Karori Library.

There are no particularly excellent cafés near where the Skyline Walkway passes. At the end in Owhiro Bay the local dairy a couple of hundred metres up Happy Valley Rd is your best bet before heading back into town. You could make a beeline for Aro Valley where there are a couple of highly recommended cafés and a deli.

At some point you will surely head into central Wellington and in Cuba St there are numerous cool cafés that await your attention. The institution Caffe L'affare in College St should guarantee you a good coffee and on a nice sunny day Parade Café on Oriental Parade is a pretty sweet spot.

 **Accommodation**

Wellington has plenty of hotels, motels and backpackers and all the things you would usually find in a big city. There is also a camping spot at Dry Creek at the eastern end of Belmont Regional Park.

**Things to do**

Wellington has loads to do on the cultural front and you really will not need much help in finding plenty of information on all of this. Te Papa is a pretty obvious choice and a good place to start. There always seems to be a festival on in Wellington, and timing a trip with this is mind is a cool idea. The city has the International Arts Festival, jazz, comedy, film and poetry festivals and many more.

You could always take an extra day and head up into Martinborough wine country while you are in town. There are plentiful vineyards, wine-tastings, restaurants and cafés, only an hour or so away from Wellington.

On a hot day in Wellington, when you are looking for a post-ride swim, Oriental Bay is the best and is really close to town, to Mt Victoria (where you can mountain bike) and Parade Café. Otherwise Scorching Bay, out near Seatoun, is a bit further afield but is famous for the Chocolate Fish Café (reportedly a favourite of many local celebrities) and is a rather cool location.

 **Other rides**

There is a truckload of other worthy rides in the Wellington area. There are other rides off Hawkins Hill with some steep and technical downhill riding. Mt Victoria in the central city is riddled with trails to explore and could be included in an urban cruise as well as other green-belt single tracks. The Akatarawa Forest has tracks including the infamous Karapoti Loop and many unmarked secret single tracks. Wainuiomata and Eastbourne also both have developing trail networks to look into.

**Contacts**

**Belmont Regional Park**: www.gw.govt.nz
**DOC Wellington**: Government Buildings, Lambton Quay, 04 472 7356
**Wellington Visitor Information Centre**: corner Wakefield and
Victoria streets, Wellington, 04 802 4860, www.wellingtonnz.com

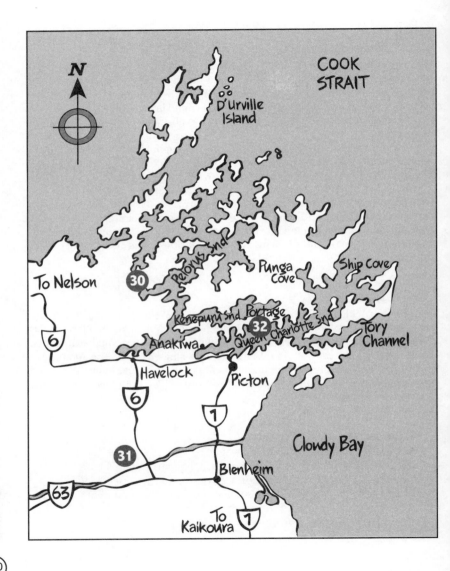

# Marlborough

**The Marlborough Sounds area has not only some of the best trail riding in the country, but also amazing scenery both in the sounds and in the hills and some of the finest food and wine around. Personally I would not limit myself to a weekend here but would rather take a week, including the Queen Charlotte Track or part of it (see page 123), add in a mountain-bike wine tour and intersperse it with some intensive relaxation.**

To make the most of your time here, organising a local transport operator to help you with the required shuttles is a great idea, and if you can include some type of water-taxi trip then getting out on the sounds adds something really special to the whole experience.

These rides are a couple of the best epic single-track rides around. For technically competent and keen mountain bikers life will not be complete until you have lapped up these trails. They are both really day-long outings, especially when you factor in the transport considerations. Each involves at least four to six hours of riding and requires more than intermediate technical skills.

Having said that, if you are keen and don't mind a bit of pushing and carrying and some walking if the roots and rocks scare you then intermediate technical riders might be tempted to give it a go. Both rides head into some reasonably remote countryside with no quick way out so you need to be self-sufficient and well prepared for injuries to both bikes and people.

# Nydia Bay Track

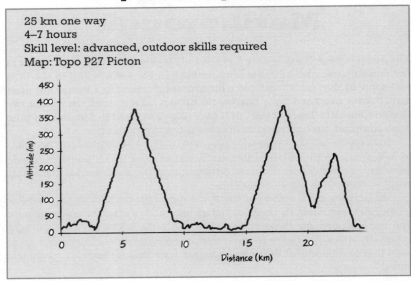

25 km one way
4–7 hours
Skill level: advanced, outdoor skills required
Map: Topo P27 Picton

The Nydia Bay Track is an epic technical single-track adventure in the stunning Marlborough Sounds. The track runs between Duncan Bay in Tennyson Inlet and Kaiuma Bay in Pelorus Sound. The riding is excellent and, apart from a couple of short sections of widened track and farmland, is all single track. There are three significant climbs to contend with and over 1000 m of total elevation gain. This is the means to the fantastic downhill riding and part of the reason to love this track. The track is challenging and technical in the dry but in the wet is a dangerous slipfest and is best avoided.

The point-to-point nature of this track means that some type of car shuttle is required if you want to do the whole thing end to end. The drive to either end of the track is on long and winding gravel roads and the ends are separated by

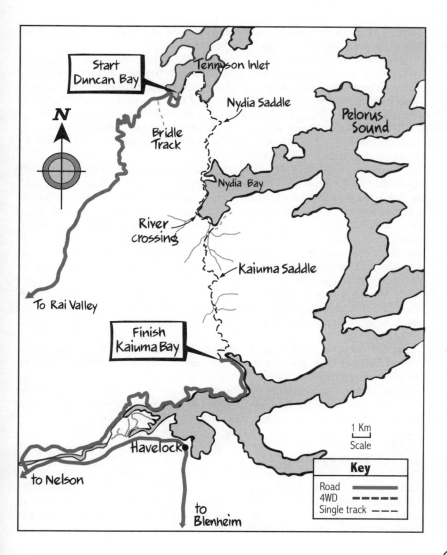

Start
Duncan Bay

Tennyson Inlet

Nydia Saddle

N

Bridle
Track

Pelorus
Sound

Nydia Bay

River
crossing

Kaiuma Saddle

To Rai Valley

Finish
Kaiuma Bay

Havelock

1 Km
Scale

to Nelson

to
Blenheim

| Key | |
| --- | --- |
| Road | |
| 4WD | |
| Single track | |

Marlborough

about 75 km. Doing your own car shuttle is an uneconomic nightmare but there are good transport options available.

Rutherford Travel in Havelock can arrange shuttle transport to and from either end of the track for small or large numbers. They use local operators and will not charge you commission. They can also arrange water-taxi transport to Shag Point at the Kaiuma Bay end, and can talk through options including boats to the Tennyson Inlet end or into and out of the halfway point at Nydia Bay.

The Rutherford Travel staff are very friendly and helpful and can also help with arrangements for the Wakamarina and Queen Charlotte tracks and all other local activities and accommodation.

There are a number of ways you can approach this track. This track description will follow the Duncan Bay (Tennyson Inlet) to Kaiuma Bay path as this is the best known and classic approach. Other options are: riding from Duncan Bay to Nydia Bay and return (24 km), no transport required; riding from Kaiuma Bay to Nydia Bay and return (24 km), again with no transport; riding from Duncan Bay to Nydia Bay and taking a boat back to Havelock; riding the track in both directions (50 km), no transport required, but it's only for those with a significant level of foolhardiness and with eight to 12 hours of consistent riding potential.

It is also worth mentioning that you can ride the track in the reverse direction from Kaiuma Bay to Duncan Bay. The general opinion is that the track is much less rideable this way but, having done it, I would suggest differently.

In this 'reverse' direction the downhill sections are less technical and almost 100 per cent rideable, better suiting less-advanced technical riders. There is a little more uphill walking to cover the steep and technical sections but you also get more of the climbing out of the way early in the ride. The views are also a little nicer in this direction and the track finishes at a delicious spot for relaxing and swimming. It is definitely worth thinking about.

**The riding**

The start of the track is at Duncan Bay in Tennyson Inlet about 30 km from State Highway 6. Just north of Rai Valley turn off to the right on Opouri Rd. Follow this until it becomes Tennyson Inlet Rd and, where that road ends, veer right into Duncans Bay Rd; continue all the way to the end past the Tennyson Inlet settlement, where the track starts.

The add-on Bridle Track from the top of Opouri Saddle at the Tennyson Inlet end is also a must-do for advanced technical riders and provides a real treat before the track proper starts.

The first part of the track is flattish and one of the rootiest sections. The track follows the coast with some views into the inlet's glorious turquoise water. There is only a small undulation along here until the first uphill to the Nydia Saddle starts in earnest at 2.7 km. The top of the saddle is at 6 km and just over 370 m in height so it is a bit of a climb. However, the gradient is nice and it is just about all rideable. The saddle is a great place for your first morning-tea stop and the views are lovely.

From the Nydia Saddle the track heads back down to sea level at Nydia Bay. The top section of this descent is by far the most rocky and technical. Don't worry if you have to walk this early stuff as things ease up considerably into technical fun track, rather then just scary rocky riding. This is a great challenge for highly skilled riders and you will appreciate having good suspension.

After a solid 3 km of concentrated rocky and rooty downhill, the track flattens into a flowing benched track and winds its way around the coast to the Nydia Bay wharf. Look out for the well-signposted pet eel pool on the way. The wharf is a worthwhile stopping spot, good for lunch and maybe a swim. This is the halfway point.

From the wharf, you continue around the edge of the water. The trail leads away on a four-wheel drive track into the trees and is mostly marked with orange arrows. The route becomes single track again and passes a few houses and Te Mahoerangi Ecolodge. After crossing a creek to the estuary the track becomes four-wheel drive again and then fords a small river (easily rideable). Follow the markers and main track close to the water until a clearly marked turn-off to Kaiuma Bay at about 14 km. Here the signs in one direction go to Nydia Lodge and in the other across farmland heading towards the end of the track, which is where you are headed.

Turn right to cross the farmland, initially passing through what looks like a corral. Follow the main four-wheel drive track straight ahead across the farmland. The markers in here can be a bit tricky to see but essentially you want to follow the main trail across the farm, passing through two small creek crossings.

You should be heading straight up the valley towards a conical hill in the foreground with a saddle on either side of it. The saddle to your left is the

Kaiuma Saddle and the one you will pass over. As the farmland starts to rise, the track veers left with a large orange marker heading into some trees.

The climb up Kaiuma Saddle is a similar height and length to the Nydia Saddle but is a combination of exposed-clay single track and familiar, cool native forest. You reach the saddle at 18 km. At the top the saddles have a very similar appearance in both directions. Again, the most technical section of the downhill is right off the top of the saddle. The native-bush rocky downhill is great fun but fairly technical riding and may require a wee bit of walking. The track doesn't drop right back to sea level but descends into exotic pines on narrow rocky trail before crossing several bridges and beginning to climb again.

The last uphill of the ride starts in pines and climbs from 75 m to 230 m. It is rocky in parts and mostly rideable except for a rock slide that is much safer walked. The gradient is steeper than the other two main saddles, or at least it feels like that by the time you get here!

From the last high point the track descends and the last 2.5 km is fun, flowing, native-bush single track. It is an all-rideable blast and a great way to finish the epic. The single track comes out on to a farm track and then on to a gravel road. Head right here and it is a kilometre back to the road-end car park.

If someone is picking you up from here, this point is accessed by heading right onto Daltons Rd 3 km north-west of Canvastown and then veering right onto Kaiuma Bay Rd and following it 24 km to the end where it meets the Nydia Track.

If you are not getting picked up here, it is 3 km on the gravel to the Shag Point boat pick-up if you are going back by water taxi, or a 27 km gravel ride back to Canvastown — but I wouldn't recommend that after such a lovely ride.

# **Wakamarina**

21 km one way
4–6 hours
Skill level: advanced, outdoor skills required
Map: Topo O28 Wairau

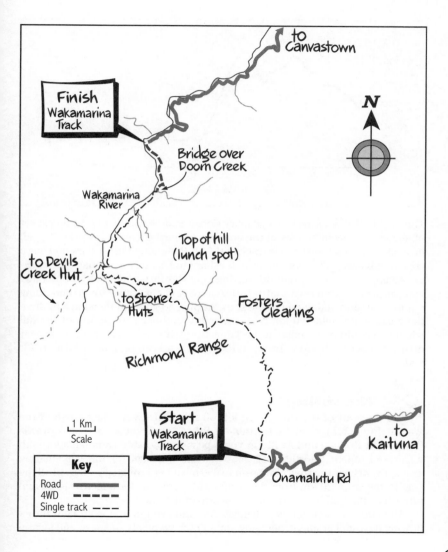

to Canvastown

N

**Finish**
Wakamarina Track

Bridge over Doom Creek

Wakamarina River

Top of hill (lunch spot)

to Devils Creek Hut

to Stone Huts

Fosters Clearing

Richmond Range

1 Km
Scale

**Start**
Wakamarina Track

to Kaituna

Onamalutu Rd

| Key | |
|-----|---|
| Road | |
| 4WD | |
| Single track | |

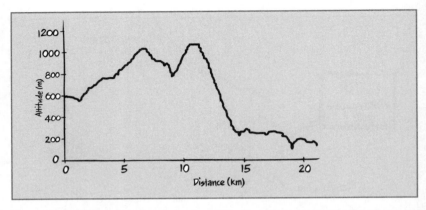

The mighty Wakamarina is a legendary ride. It contains arguably the nicest set of single-track switchbacks in the country, or maybe even the world. It is all lush native beech forest single track in the Mt Richmond Forest Park and has a considerable overall elevation drop. It is hard to beat as a personal favourite.

Again, as a point-to-point ride having a car shuttle is a necessity. Potentially you can arrange your own shuttle by leaving one car at Canvastown (and riding out to here) and taking one to the start. At the end you will then have to drive the winding gravelled 20 km from the main road back to the top of the hill when you could be relaxing at the Trout Hotel. If you haven't got a volunteer driver contact Rutherford Travel in Havelock who can organise transport for you.

## The riding

To find the start of the track, turn left off State Highway 6 just north of the Wairau River bridge on to Northbank Rd. After 5 km veer right towards Onamalutu Domain and at 12 km you'll pass this notable camping spot with water and toilets. Shortly after this veer left at a sign for the Wakamarina Track. From here the road climbs up to 600 m and is a rough gravel road all the way to the start, 20 km from the main road. Look out for a sharp right-hand turn-off to the trail-head car park at the top of the hill.

The start of the track is a delight. The first section jumps straight into a flowing downhill gradient, allowing you to pick up plenty of speed and swoop around the corners. You can't help but smile. After about 1.5 km, with all that enthusiasm, you hit some short, steep uphills that feel like a bit of a strain. After this, things flatten out a little bit and the gradient becomes a bit more reasonable before the real climb up to Fosters Clearing begins.

It is a total of 6.6 km to the clearing, which is the first of two high points on the ride, at 1041 m. The track is all rideable up to here, a little bumpy and rocky in places but well benched and drained since DOC controversially upgraded some of the track several years ago. Fosters Clearing is a nice place for a snack stop. There is a side trip up to Fosters Hut if you are keen on a bit of a push up and a lush single track down.

From the clearing the track heads down for 2.5 km and drops by about 250 m; it is all good fun and not too technical until you hit a taste of switchbacks and head down to a creek crossing at 9 km. From this point to the second high point is just about all upwards and almost entirely non-rideable. Be prepared to push your bike or carry it on your shoulder for the next 2 km as you slog your way back to 1075 m. It is slow and draining but luckily well worth it.

You will come out into an obvious clearing at 11 km, just as the track has sidled around the top of the hill. This is a perfect lunch spot, a welcome rest and a necessary reviver to gather your wits and strength for the descent. In the old-worldy forest this is often a sunny spot for a break.

From this point things are sensationally technical and rooty to start with. The track heads away from the clearing and you need to remember to watch for the markers as well as concentrate on the riding. There is one point within minutes of the top where the track appears to lead you right but the markers head left and you could easily lose the track. The beech-forest surface is clay and rocks covered in a thick layer of cornflake-like leaves with roots crossing all over the show. The top is the most technical section so if you find it hard going, remember that things ease up as you head towards the switchbacks and become less seriously bumpy.

Down, down, down you go. Things don't get much better than this 800 vertical metres of solid descent. Frequent breaks to regroup, hoot and laugh excitedly and let your brakes cool off are a good idea. At the bottom of the main descent a track heads off to Stone Huts and you continue to the right, passing the Devil's Creek Hut turn-off as well.

The next 4.5 km undulates above the Wakamarina River. The track is in lush forest and is fun and flowing. At 19 km you will come to a long rocky downhill, which you may choose not to ride, and a bridge crossing Doom

Creek. A nasty uphill may temporarily wipe the smile off your face but it isn't long and from here it is only 2 km of rolling four-wheel drive track to the car park at the end of Wakamarina Rd.

If you are being picked up here, access is by turning into Wakamarina Rd at the Trout Hotel in Canvastown and following it to the end. Easy. If you are riding back to Canvastown it is a relatively painless 15 km on the road but doesn't add a lot of joy to the ride.

Note: A great option if you don't want to do the shuttle is to ride up and back to the high point from the far end. There is a bit of pushing for sure but the best of the downhill follows.

 **Coffee and food**

It is likely that you will pass through Havelock with either of these rides, and you can get food there. There is a well-stocked Four Square supermarket and a decent bakery with fresh pastries. There is a café here on the main road which is OK but the Slip Inn at the marina is a nice choice. If you are looking for a post-ride feed the Sounds Like Kaff has reasonable fish and chips and the mussel restaurant may be worth a stop while you are in the 'green-lipped mussel capital of the world'.

The Clansman restaurant and bar, also on the main road, has a nice atmosphere and pretty good food. For real pub atmosphere and food you can't go past the Trout Hotel at Canvastown and it is a traditional stopping point following a ride on the Wakamarina. Be warned that Rai Valley on the way to Nydia Bay has a pretty limited food selection and it pays to be stocked up before getting here.

Of course if you are planning to head towards Blenheim before or after either of these rides then the fine wine and food selection increases off the scale. Many of the local wineries have restaurants open for lunch and some are also open in the evenings. Blenheim itself has the typical fast-food options and some great restaurants as well as numerous supermarkets. Living Room (corner Scott St and Maxwell Rd) has good coffee. If you happen to be in Blenheim in the cherry season it would be rude not to take advantage of the amazing fruit they have here. Most of the orchards and gate sales are on State Highway 6 near Blenheim and Rapaura Rd.

# Accommodation

If you intend to stay in Blenheim or Havelock there are numerous accommodation options. Blenheim has a multitude of upmarket boutique lodges, B&Bs and cottages around the vineyard areas. Vintners Retreat Resort is an amazing base with house-sized accommodation. Havelock is a little more subdued in its costs with Havelock Garden Motel, and a YHA hostel in the renovated old school, and the Trout Hotel in Canvastown is a very affordable option with its two motel units and old-style hotel rooms.

Along the Nydia Track it is worth knowing about the Te Mahoerangi Ecolodge backpackers in Nydia Bay, which comes recommended for its relaxed style and location. If you have a large group riding the Nydia Track it is worth investigating the DOC Nydia Lodge (in Nydia Bay), which sleeps four to 50 and has full facilities including hot showers.

For those who like the camping there are two great spots associated with the Wakamarina Track. The Onamalutu Domain is a large grassy and tree-surrounded area for free camping with basic facilities. It is on the way to the start and is 12 km from the main road. The campsite just below the car park at the far end of the Wakamarina Track is great. A couple of sites tucked away at the end have fire facilities and access to swimming holes in the river and in my opinion are the icing on the cake after this ride.

 # Things to do

Swimming at Duncan Bay or Nydia Bay are great options when you are out riding. If you are looking for a swimming spot in the Wakamarina River then sneak down from the campsite at the far end of the track or anywhere you can get to the river up this end of the valley. The Wairau River on the way back to Blenheim may be a good spot as long as the water levels haven't been sucked down by a drought. If you're heading towards Nelson the Pelorus River is always a good place for a dip too.

## Contacts

**DOC office Havelock**: c/o Rutherford Travel, see below
**Havelock Garden Motel**: Main Rd, Havelock, 03 574 2387, www.gardenmotels.com

**Rutherford Travel**: 46 Main Rd, Havelock, 03 574 2114, www.rutherfordtravel.co.nz (for transport and accommodation help)
**Trout Hotel**: Main Rd, Canvastown, 03 574 2888
**Vintners Retreat Resort**: Raupara Rd, Blenheim, 03 572 7420, www.thevintnersretreat.co.nz

# Queen Charlotte Sound

**The Queen Charlotte Track from Ship Cove to Anakiwa in the Marlborough Sounds is the country's best-known multi-day single-track mountain-bike ride. The track has spectacular coastal scenery and beaches, lush single-track riding and the excitement and challenge of being a two- or three-day trip. It is a perfectly contained long weekend away. It is also a shining example of the effective management of a popular dual-use track and one that is often cited in the lobbying for mountain-biking access to other tracks.**

Some people do ride the track in one day but this leaves little time for relaxing and enjoying the surroundings. Two days is a viable option but most people who do this cut out a large section of single track in the middle from Kenepuru Saddle to Te Mahia in favour of riding on the road. With a three-day trip you can ride the complete track (and decide for yourself how you feel about the middle section); you can also have plenty of down-time at your stopping points to appreciate the amazing locations and you have the option of cruising back to Picton via the Queen Charlotte Drive by bike.

# Queen Charlotte Track

Skill level: intermediate
Map: Topo P27 Picton

**Day 1:** Ship Cove to Punga Cove — 24.5 km (2–4 hours)
**Day 2:** Punga Cove to Portage — 22.5 km (3–5 hours)
**Day 3:** Portage to Anakiwa and Picton — 17.5 km (2–3 hours to Anakiwa) and 24 km (1–2 hours) to Picton

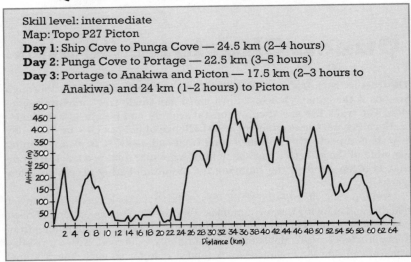

From a technical point of view the Queen Charlotte Track is accessible to most mountain bikers. For the main part it is a reasonably wide benched single track with few technically challenging obstacles. Having said this, the flowing nature of the trail, the location and terrain mean that skilled riders will still find plenty of interest here.

From a length point of view the track requires reasonable fitness and familiarity with spending time in the saddle. (It's 65 km from Ship Cove to Anakiwa and 24 km from Anakiwa to Picton via Queen Charlotte Drive.)

The far end of the track from Ship Cove to Camp Bay/Punga Cove Resort is closed to bikes from 1 December to 28 February to avoid user conflict during the popular holiday season.

**The riding**

A little bit of organisation is required for a trip on the Queen Charlotte Track. You need to get from Picton to the start of the track at Ship Cove by boat, organise transport of your luggage (spare clothes and food) unless you fancy carrying it the whole way, and arrange accommodation at your stopping points. You also need to decide how you will return to Picton from the end of the track at Anakiwa.

My suggestion is to arrange the water taxi from Picton to Ship Cove for as early in the morning as possible and use the same company to transport your luggage so you can carry just a small day pack. Plan to do the trip in three days and to stay the first night somewhere in Endeavour Inlet, probably towards Punga Cove, and the second night at Portage or Te Mahia. It is an easy 24 km along the Queen Charlotte Drive back to Picton and riding this is a reasonable option unless you can leave a spare car here.

The Queen Charlotte Track is clearly marked the whole way. There are a few side trips to bays and beaches and a couple of points that the track crosses roads where you need to keep an eye on it, but otherwise the navigation is simple.

The track passes through a mixture of DOC and private land and unless a diversion is marked you must stay on the track.

## Day 1: Ship Cove to Punga Cove

From the Ship Cove wharf the track heads off to your left. The initial climb out of Ship Cove is a harsh start to the track but one that will get you fairly quickly warmed up and only lasts 20 minutes or so. The section following this is one of the nicest parts of the track. It is benched single track that winds its way through the native bush with stunning views of the small inlets of the outer sounds. Over the first saddle the track drops gradually down to Resolution Bay. From here it is a more gradual climb up and over the Tawa Saddle to the edge of Endeavour Inlet. The track follows the shoreline, passing Furneaux Lodge at the head of the inlet and then continues winding near the edge of the water past Big Bay and then to Camp Bay and Punga Cove. If you are not stopping, head right at the junction before Punga Cove. If you are staying at Punga Cove, head left.

The accommodation options at this point are camping at the DOC Camp Bay campsite, Punga Cove Resort or Mahana Homestead.

## Day 2: Punga Cove to Portage

From Punga Cove the track heads up to the Kenepuru Saddle, then continues up and along the undulating tops to the Torea Saddle where it meets the road to Portage. The track through this section is steep in parts and is quite exposed and very hot in summer. Parts of this will feel like a grind with the view the only real consolation. Some people who have already ridden the Queen Charlotte Track opt to ride on the road to Torea Saddle and avoid this section. Despite that it is hard work, it is well worth doing it to get a feel for the whole track — you can ride on the road anytime! Take your time, enjoy the view, stop at the shelters along the way and feel vindicated when you relax with an exhausted grin at your accommodation.

From Kenepuru Saddle the track climbs over three high points in 10 km; the last one is the highest on the ride. From the high point the track continues to undulate over another three peaks in 12 km but has an overall elevation loss. The ups and downs remain steep in places and will be challenging to those with less fitness. The final downhill to Torea Saddle is great fun and will leave you with a smile. When the track hits Torea Rd turn right to head to Portage if this is where you are staying. Or, if you are continuing on to Te Mahia, be prepared that the climbing is not yet over with (see next section).

Accommodation options at Portage are the Portage Resort Hotel, the Portage Bay Shop and Backpackers and the DOC Cowshed Bay campsite a little further along the road. Te Mahia has a lovely resort if you can face one more big climb to get there.

## Day 3: Portage to Anakiwa and Picton

From Portage you need to head back up the road and return to the point you exited the track. From the Torea Saddle there is sadly a reasonable sort of climb of about 300 m to start the day. However, what goes up must come down and the descent to Te Mahia Saddle makes up for it all.

The James Vogel Track, which is a diversion off to the left of the main track just before Te Mahia, drops down to Mistletoe Bay. It is a favourite little extra treat for advanced riders fond of very technical single track. It is tricky beech-forest riding at its best.

The actual Queen Charlotte Track doesn't go down to Mistletoe Bay but a gravel road from the saddle does and it is a nice place for a scenic stop and a swim. If you have detoured to Mistletoe Bay you need to climb back out of here via the gravel road.

The track continues, heading off to the left just before the main road. It passes into a short section of farmland single track with views to the hills near Picton. When the track heads back into the native bush, the lush single-track finale begins. There is a little bit of a climb but once you start descending be assured that pretty much all of the last 7 km is a blissful downhill gradient with swooping corners and divine views. This is a popular part of the track so be careful of walkers who may be lurking around blind corners. There is a very short uphill just after Davies Bay but it is pretty easy going and prepares you for a final run down to Anakiwa.

If you are planning to ride back to Picton, head out of Anakiwa and turn left at Queen Charlotte Dr. The road undulates around the water's edge from here.

## Coffee and food

Along the track numerous lodges provide food and drinks for both guests and passing bikers and walkers. Furneaux Lodge has a great bar and restaurant and could well be your first morning-tea or lunch stop. Some people have been known to stop here for a beer mid-morning too. Punga Cove Resort has a well-known fine-dining restaurant and a more casual café, both of which serve excellent food. There is nowhere to stop in the mid-section of the track and no water available either. Portage Resort has a flash restaurant and you can get groceries or takeaways at the store.

## Accommodation

Bookings for accommodation should definitely be made in advance. In summer it pays to book early and in winter check if the restaurant and meal facilities are operating.

DOC's Camp Bay campsite has water and toilets (small fee required).

Punga Cove (www.pungacove.co.nz) has a range of options from backpackers to luxury accommodation and you can self-cater or dine at the lovely restaurant.

Mahana Homestead (www.mahanahomestead.com) has lodge-style accommodation with meals and self-catering facilities. The Portage Resort Hotel (www.portage.co.nz) has dorm-style and upmarket accommodation. Also in

Portage is Portage Bay Shop and Backpackers (www.portagecharters.co.nz).

DOC's Cowshed Bay campsite is slightly further west past Portage on the road (small fee required).

Te Mahia Bay Resort (www.temahia.co.nz) has a variety of accommodation in a beautiful little bay.

## Contacts

**General track information**: www.qctrack.co.nz

**Picton visitor information centre**: The Foreshore, Picton, 03 520 3113, www.destinationmarlborough.com

The main water-transport providers for taking you to the start and transporting your luggage are:

**Arrow Water Taxis**: 03 573 8229

**Cougar Line**: 03 573 7925, www.queencharlottetrack.co.nz

**Endeavour Express**: 03 573 5456

There are some regular daily runs with several suitable morning departure times in summer and a less frequent timetable in the off season (May to September), though some services operate on demand.

# Golden Bay

**Golden Bay is beautiful. As soon as you drive up and then over the Takaka Hill you enter another world, with a relaxing pace of life, great weather and a very nice style. The scenery in Golden Bay is exceptional, the beaches golden and verging on tropical and of course the mountain biking is a unique, amazing experience! There are also some exceptional spots for hanging out, for pre- and post-ride refuelling, and plenty of other exploring to do. A weekend will only just get you started!**

There is a lot of riding to be done in the Golden Bay area; this weekend takes in the best of the single-track trail riding but if you are looking for other adventures the Quiet Revolution Cycle Shop has produced *The Mountain Biker's Guide to Golden Bay*, which is available from the bike shop or information centre.

Depending on which way you do the Rameka Track, it can be suitable for all mountain bikers and has 6 km of divine native-bush trail that everyone will love. The Kill Devil is definitely a ride for advanced riders, and you have to be reasonably fit as the uphill will put off many. However, the single track is simply fantastic and it is an absolutely stunning ride unlike any other. For a little fun exploration on some local after-work type trails, Parapara is a cool tightly crafted network of tracks that are suitable for everyone and make a good stop when heading further out into the bay for a look around.

With anticipation we wait for the review of mountain biking on the Heaphy Track and hope Golden Bay will be the gateway to this amazing ride again. It is also possible that some other areas will become accessible to mountain bikes through this process and in the meantime DOC assures me that at least some of the Flora car park to Barron Flat ride is not legal. Fingers crossed.

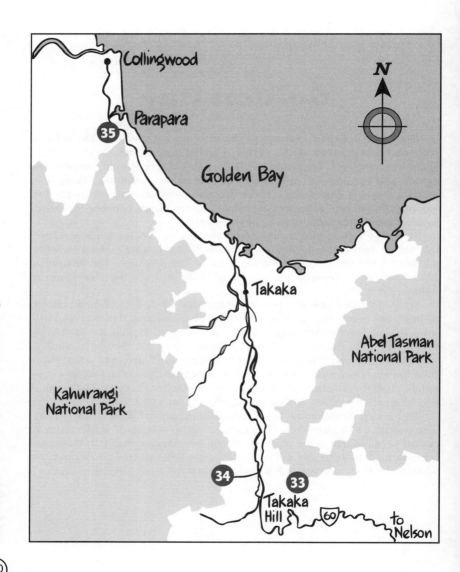

# Rameka Track

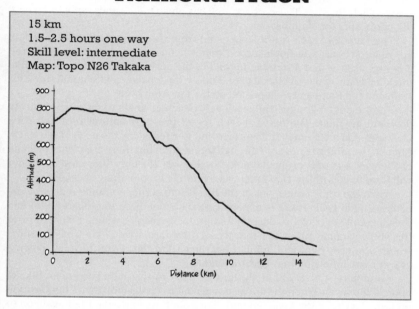

15 km
1.5–2.5 hours one way
Skill level: intermediate
Map: Topo N26 Takaka

The Rameka Track is a fairly short but very sweet treat of a ride in the otherwise off-limits Abel Tasman National Park. As part of an old pack track, the Rameka has maintained its status as a paper road, and therefore mountain biking is permitted on it. The lush single-track section of the ride is about 6 km long with the remainder of downhill gravel road. The Rameka Track is suitable for most keen mountain bikers as the single track is a relaxed gradient with no dangerous obstacles. There are several options for riding the Rameka Track depending on your fitness level, transport options and inclination. The option described is for a one-way ride down the track with car shuttle or pick-up from the end.

**Golden Bay**

**The riding**

The start of the Rameka track is at the end of Canaan Rd, a gravel road off to your right just short of the top of Takaka Hill. From the turn-off, the road end and car park area is 11 km away. This is also the access point for a visit to Harwoods Hole cave. The car park area has plush toilets and water and plenty of opportunity for camping out.

The Rameka Track is not signposted from the car park and the map and information board was not in a good state when I was recently there. However, it is very easy to find. From the far end of the parking area a four-wheel drive track leads away past a closed gate. Follow this grassy, gentle uphill track for 1 km and the Rameka is signposted on the left from here.

For the next 5 km the trail is a lovely benched single track with a delicate downhill gradient. The native beech forest provides natural root and rock obstacles and a very nice trail surface and low ferns line the edge of the track. Almost everything is rideable through this section but there are plenty of small challenges. A couple of small creek crossings are the only things a skilled rider will have to get off for. Don't rush, as the forest is something special.

When the track comes out of the forest into scrub, continue following the obvious main trail. There is a steep rutted section here to be careful on and then a couple of tricky rocky bits that probably require walking. Shortly after this you will come out on to a four-wheel drive farm road (7 km from the start) where you veer right and uphill. Less than 1 km further on turn left down a gravel road, following the signs for Takaka.

From here it is downhill all the way back to the main road near Takaka about 7 km away. When the gravel comes out to civilisation at a T intersection on Rameka Creek Rd, head left and then a short distance later left again on to an unnamed sealed road. At the end of this turn right into Central Takaka Rd, which will take you to State Highway 60, the main road to Takaka.

A similar-duration ride, and probably the nicest way to maximise single track and minimise fuss, is to ride the track down to the end of the forest and then turn around and return the same way. The gradient back up is really very nice. Alternatively, if you don't mind a climb of 750 m, you could ride from Takaka to the top of the hill via the Rameka Track and then back down. The other option, which includes riding up the Takaka Hill by road, is entirely possible but not a good one!

# Kill Devil

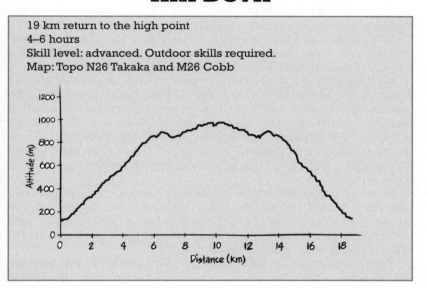

19 km return to the high point
4–6 hours
Skill level: advanced. Outdoor skills required.
Map: Topo N26 Takaka and M26 Cobb

Kill Devil is an amazing ride. It is a rocky technical challenge both up and downhill and a significant 840 m elevation gain. The scenery is amazing and the Lockett Range you ride on borders the Kahurangi National Park. This is not a ride for the faint-hearted; the climb up the Kill Devil Spur takes around two hours and, after a ride along the tops, the downward route is a brake-burning, switchback-riddled bone-shaking good time. It is a ride suited to technical, energetic riders with reasonable outdoor skills.

## The riding
To get to the start of the Kill Devil Track, head towards Takaka from the bottom

of the Takaka Hill for 6 km and turn left into Uruwhenua Rd. After 3 km turn right into what looks like someone's driveway (there may or may not be a track sign as it seemed to have been knocked over last time I was there). Follow this road through a gate and keep an eye out for orange markers, veering left at a fork to the parking area 4 km from the main road. Car parking is limited here and don't park in the road as it is someone's driveway. The signage in general for this track is pretty scant.

At the parking area there is a small shelter with an intentions book. From here the track is obvious and heads down to a dry stream crossing before a real stream crossing and the start of the uphill.

For 6 km and 750 vertical metres the track goes up. The climbing gradient is actually very pleasant due to more than 50 switchbacks. A majority of the climb is easily rideable, with the rocky acute-angle corners providing most of the technical challenge on the climb. The track is initially in low bush but as it climbs becomes more open and exposed. The view gets more impressive as you go up; first you see the Takaka Valley, then out to the Golden Bay coast and when you get to the top you'll look into the Waingaro River valley and Kahurangi National Park.

As the switchbacks come to an end the track climbs a little more, has a wee nasty rutted downhill and then reaches an obvious rock viewing platform. This is a nice place to stop for lunch. The views from here are superb; to your right the terrain drops away steeply in bluffs to the river below and the contoured bush-clad valley seems to go on forever.

From the viewing spot, the track drops, with a couple of tricky sections, and sidles below the ridge line on some testing rocky terrain. After a short uphill you come back to the ridge and from here effectively follow the tops. This part of the track should really be undulating but actually has an uphill gradient, and the high point in the ride is yet to come. In this section of track you will pass a side track on the left leading to a newly renovated historic hut — it is well worth a look or a snack stop. After a short downhill section another large rock on the right side of the track makes an excellent viewing spot. This is the high point and turn-around spot as described.

From this point it is another hour or so to Riordan's Hut. The track drops, climbs to a saddle and then branches off to the left towards the hut. A short section just after the turn-off is unrideable but after this the track is reasonably good. It is well worth the ride into the historic musterer's hut to have a look, or even to stay the night. Riordan's Hut borders the Kahurangi National Park so riding further than this point is out of bounds. If you chose to return from the high point of the track, the total distance is 19 km and the trip is about four to five hours. If you go all the way to Riordan's Hut expect it to take about four to five hours to get there and 2.5–3.5 hours to get back. Both options follow the same route out. Remember that the altitude makes you particularly vulnerable to the weather and it can get mightily cold if the weather closes in. Be prepared for alpine conditions.

# Parapara Trails

1–2 hours of playing
Skill level: all
Map: Mountain Biker's Guide to Golden Bay

The Wakatu Forestry block at Parapara has a sweet, tight collection of hand-built single track worth checking out for an hour or two. The trails are fun with plenty of little challenges and follow the natural features of the land through some interesting terrain. This is a place suitable for most mountain bikers and you could bring your family for a little scoot in here too.

 **The riding**

The Parapara mountain-bike trails are 19 km north-west of Takaka on State Highway 60. Follow the main road from Takaka towards Farewell Spit. When the road crosses the Parapara Inlet, you will see a forestry block on your left on the far side of the inlet. Park on the side of the road before the bridge over the Parapara River. The basic map of the trails in this area (and others in Golden Bay) is available from the Quiet Revolution Cycle Shop or the visitor information centre in Takaka.

Many of the tracks are marked once you get into the trail system, and the area is small enough that you can't really get lost anyway. The block is basically bordered by the inlet to your left and by the Parapara River, which also loops behind the forest block, to your right. There are two main entry points to the trails. One is just to the side of the inlet — head towards Takaka and the trail is on the right over a chain-link fence. This follows a flat track before heading uphill on some cool zigzags before reaching a four-wheel drive track that runs down the middle of the area. If you take this option, turn left on to this and near the pond you will meet up with a collection of other single-track trails.

For the other entry point, ride towards the bridge and take the four-wheel drive track on your left for only a few metres before the single track branches off to the right. The track is easy to follow in here and there are all sorts of short named bits of trail including a trip to a sweet swimming hole in the river. If you want to play around in here for a bit you will end up riding things repeatedly but it is all just a bit of good old local riding fun on some well-loved and looked-after trails.

 **Coffee and food**

Golden Bay has no shortage of good food, with an emphasis on quality and wholesome local produce. The Wholemeal Café in Takaka's main street is an institution, open for all meals and with excellent coffee and a lot of room. Golden Fries, also in Takaka, is reputedly an excellent chippie. The Mussel Inn halfway between Takaka and Collingwood is also a widely appreciated spot, serving the local product and brewing its own beverages. A little further out, the Courthouse Café in Collingwood is good too and there's a coffee shop in Pohara. The Farewell Spit café has the most amazing views and home cooking. If you are heading that far afield, the Awaroa Lodge café on the Abel Tasman Track from Totaranui is stunning. Takaka also has a new flash, well-stocked supermarket. And lastly, when you pass through Motueka a stop at Hot Mamas for coffee or a feed any time is traditional.

 **Accommodation**

There are plenty of options for accommodation, with camping, B&Bs and backpackers the most prolific. You can camp at Harwoods Hole/Rameka Track Rd end, where there is water and toilets. Takaka has the Paynes Ford Hangdog Camp, a relaxed and well-equipped spot, and it also has numerous backpackers and several motels. The next-closest camping ground is at Pohara. The Sans

Souci Inn in Pohara has more upmarket accommodation and food.

On the Kill Devil Track, Riordan's Hut was renovated by DOC in 2003 and restored in keeping with its historic character. It has three bunks, a fireplace and a camp oven. The hut is very cool but basic rather than luxurious. It does not require hut tickets.

## Things to do

There is a lot to do in Golden Bay and a weekend will not do it justice, especially if it is already filled with the great mountain biking. For starters, before you ride the Rameka Track you should take the 30-minute walk to Harwoods Hole, the biggest cave in the Southern Hemisphere at 400 m deep. It appeared in *The Lord of the Rings*. After a ride down the Rameka, a dip in the excellent swimming hole at Paynes Ford is a great idea and it's signposted off the main road Bring your climbing gear too if you are keen on that as it is a well-regarded spot.

There are numerous beaches to explore in Golden Bay and the Abel Tasman — Wainui Beach at the end of the Abel Tasman is lovely and nice for swimming and Totaranui is stunning, has good camping and you can walk to Awaroa Lodge but it's a bit of a drive. There are a number of beaches to swim at on the way to Farewell Spit but they are quite tidal. Wharariki on the west coast is stunning and it's a great walk out there but it's not recommended for swimming due to its strong currents. There is also the amazing Waikoropupu Springs, New Zealand's largest freshwater spring — but don't get excited about swimming here as it is not permitted and is very cold water indeed.

Tramping and walking options in Golden Bay abound and there is everything from an hour-long wander to a five-day tramp if you want to include pedestrian activities. The Abel Tasman and Kahurangi national parks have endless options and these are nice to see on foot because you can't ride here. Kahurangi Point is a possibility if you have a spare couple of days and you can bike here if you don't mind riding on the beach and a big river crossing. The route goes from Anatori to Kahurangi Point via Big River and there is a DOC house to stay in.

Sea kayaking is the other obvious recreational choice in this area of the country and the Abel Tasman is a classic and divinely beautiful spot. Most of the rental and trip opportunities are based at the Marahau end of the park.

## Contacts
**DOC Takaka office**: 62 Commercial St, Takaka, 03 525 8026
**Takaka visitor information centre**: Willow St, Takaka, 03 525 9136
**The Quiet Revolution Cycle Shop**: 11 Commercial St, Takaka, 03 525 9555

# Nelson

Everyone knows that Nelson is lovely. For mountain bikers it is ever lovelier because you can ride numerous great trails right from town. The range of sweet single track is fantastic. There are trip options from an hour or two to a whole day, and then there are the rides just a little further afield in Marlborough or Golden Bay. A real advantage of Nelson is that it backs onto the Mt Richmond Forest Park, which is accessible to mountain bikes, and local authorities seem to have a positive approach to riding. Nelson also has a strong mountain-biking community that is building and expanding the local trail system. The other great things about a trip away to Nelson are the generally sunny weather, nice beaches and rivers, great food and drink and a wide range of things to do.

Obviously you could spend a lot of time in Nelson, biking, drifting around and generally having fun. A weekend or long weekend here does not do the local riding justice. However, in just a couple of days this selection of trail riding will ensure you have sampled some of the sweetest around.

The ride to Coppermine Saddle will suit many riders. It incorporates the very cruisy ride up the Dun Mountain Trail and then adds on some lush beech forest and sub-alpine trail for more skilled riders. Likewise the Hackett Track starts with some easy single track and then gets increasingly technical to Browning Hut. This provides options for groups of differing skill levels and the beautiful scenery means that even if you do have to walk a little you will still have a great time.

The new Peaking Ridge Track will provide a challenge to advanced technical riders who like rooty terrain but the first climb will test their fitness.

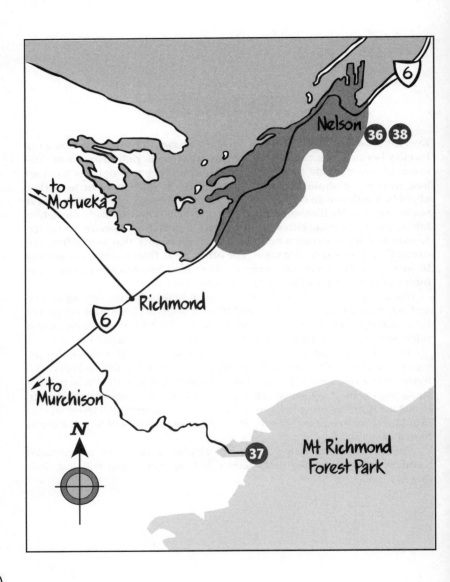

# Coppermine Saddle

33 km return
3–5 hours
Skill level: recreational to Third House; intermediate beyond
    Third House
Map: Topo O27 Nelson

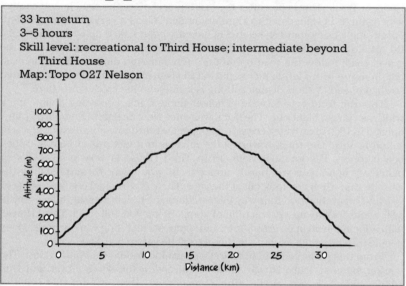

The ride to Coppermine Saddle via the Dun Mountain Track is sensational and accessible right from the centre of Nelson. It incorporates the Dun Mountain Track to Third House, which is a popular easy-gradient non-technical single track that, although pleasant in itself, is very much improved by extending the trip to Coppermine Saddle. Between Third House and Coppermine Saddle the riding is more technical and a much more interesting combination of beech forest and rocky alpine trail, with sensational views back towards Nelson and into the Richmond Ranges.

**The riding**

Most definitely the nicest way to get up to the Dun Mountain Track is via Codgers Track. From Nelson East, follow Brook St up the valley and about 10 m before Blick Tce on your right is a gravel track on your left, known as Codgers Track. This is just after the last house, before the road becomes two-way again. It is signposted to Dun Mountain. This is a very pleasant gradient uphill single track that has relatively recently been linked up to the Tantragee Rd to allow access to this trail. When this single track comes out on to the gravel road, follow the road uphill for a few hundred metres. The main road continues up with a left-hand hairpin but the Dun Mountain Track is signposted straight ahead. A short distance along is a gate and the track starts here.

The trail from here is wide benched single track, becoming double-track width as you get higher up. The track was once New Zealand's first railway line, opened in 1862 to provide access to a copper and chromite mine, with a gradient suited to this. The track traverses the hillside in a mixture of pine and then beech forest. The gradient right up to Third House is very genteel. It's so painlessly uphill you will hardly notice it but you might be surprised by the altitude gain when you look out at the view. There is a bridged creek crossing or two and other than two four-way intersections the trail is pleasantly uneventful as it winds its way up. After a total of about 10 km you will reach Third House, with a shelter in an open grassy area and signposts directing you onwards. Many people turn around here, but continuing will be very rewarding.

From this point you will head to Coppermine Saddle via Windy Point. The marker signs at Third House show the direction for Windy Point and Dun Saddle, which is the saddle after Coppermine. Head off on this track, a narrower and slightly more technical version of what you have come up. It is lovely, lush beech-forest riding and the gradient remains fairly easy. The track remains obvious the whole way but has some more technical and rocky sections as you come out into the semi-alpine open. Some short walking sections may be required but it is mostly fun riding, if a little chilly at times.

Windy Point at 15 km is just that, a windy point. It is also a junction with some walking tracks. From here Coppermine Saddle is signposted in the same direction as Dun Saddle and is a further 1.5 km of rocky alpine riding with spectacular views. It is a lot of fun.

When you reach Coppermine Saddle you will turn around and follow your tyre tracks back the way you have come. It is obviously all downhill from here and you get to enjoy the technical challenges first followed by the cruisy, pedal-free gradient of the Dun Mountain Track from Third House.

Keep your ear to the ground as the Nelson City Council is currently building a single track that will eventually lead from the Coppermine Saddle to the Maitai Dam. It may well be finished by the time you get there.

Mt Richmond Forest Park has plenty of other sensational mountain-bike riding. For experienced, skilled and fit riders looking for a full-day adventure, the ride from Coppermine Saddle to Rocks and Midi huts and out via the Pelorus River is outstanding.

# Hackett Track
# to Browning Hut

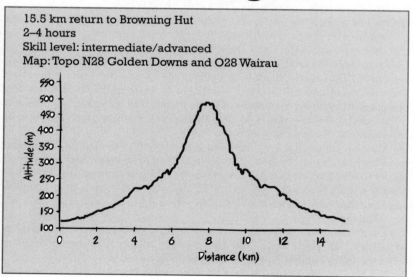

15.5 km return to Browning Hut
2–4 hours
Skill level: intermediate/advanced
Map: Topo N28 Golden Downs and O28 Wairau

The Hackett Valley in the Mt Richmond Forest Park has some very sweet mountain-bike riding. The single-track ride to Browning Hut makes for a great little adventure and it's a sensational and challenging ride back down from the hut. The other riding options from this track make it a suitable place to bring less-experienced technical riders who may want to enjoy the Whispering Falls Track or head to Hackett Hut. These tracks also make a nice walk if you have non-riders along.

 ## The riding

To get to the start of the Hackett Track from Nelson, follow the signs for Richmond and Hope. When you're 5 km south of Richmond on State Highway 6 turn left and follow the Aniseed Valley Rd for 12 km and over the hill to the Hackett picnic area. Here there is a parking area and good river swimming under the bridge.

From the car park, head over the main river bridge and turn right. Follow this track on to the gravel road and continue straight ahead as the road seems to turn left. Shortly you will come to a swing bridge and river ford. When the river is low, riding or walking across the ford is a good option as these swing bridges are a bit of a pain with a bike. A double track leads away from the river and shortly after this the single track begins.

From here the trail is easy to follow and all the intersections are well signposted. Initially the track is an open, graded single track above the river. The surface is covered in small rocks but is easily rideable and has few obstacles. After about 15 minutes of single track a trail is marked off to the left to Whispering Falls — this is an easy single track to a waterfall viewing spot and is suitable for less experienced riders.

After 4.8 km the track to Browning Hut veers off to the left (and the right-hand track heads directly to the Hackett Hut). The trail is grassy here and slightly harder to see at the very start; the sign may be a little overgrown also. From this point the track becomes more technical. You will soon cross a river and then head into the trees. The track is rockier in here and some technical sections will be a challenge.

After a kilometre or so you will reach another intersection. Here the right-hand track also leads to Hackett Hut, forming a loop. You should continue onwards to Browning Hut by following the left-hand track.

Not far along from here is a tricky river crossing where you head slightly up the river and then up a steep bank on the right. This is definitely a challenge to carry a bike up. There is a 'flood path' but I hear it is a nightmare and should only be taken in exceptional circumstances (in which case you probably shouldn't be here!).

The track continues climbing up towards Browning Hut. There are increasing numbers of rocky and rooty obstacles and short steeper sections. Things become quite a challenge but it is fun to try to clear these sections. You should probably expect some walking in this part.

At 7.8 km you need to veer right at an unmarked single-track intersection, which is not far from the hut. Browning Hut is a basic DOC hut with eight bunks. It makes a nice spot for lunch and has views into the surrounding Richmond Ranges. There is a toilet here but no tap water.

From the hut you head back the way you have come — be prepared to enjoy the challenging but very rideable downhill. Pinch-flats are popular on these rocks so go easy and make sure you have a spare tube. Back in the beech forest things ease up technically and you head back to the nasty river crossing. After this the trail is rideable just about the whole way home. The last section beside the river is relaxed and flowing and has a very pleasant downhill bias.

Another popular riding option is to do a loop to the Hackett Hut. The trail is less technical and shorter than the ride to Browning Hut. To take this option, at the track intersection 4.8 km from the start you head straight ahead, following the signs to Hackett Hut, which is at about 6 km.

After stopping for a break you can either head back the way you came or go past the hut, cross a creek and rejoin the Browning Hut Track. When you reach this intersection turn left and head down for a kilometre until you reach the intersection with the main track again. Here, turn right to head back to the car park.

This area is popular with walkers so you need to be on the lookout for pedestrians the whole way, particularly on the section beside the Hackett Creek. Back at the car park make sure you stop for a swim in the beautiful river if the weather is good, and make use of the generous picnic space.

# Peaking Ridge

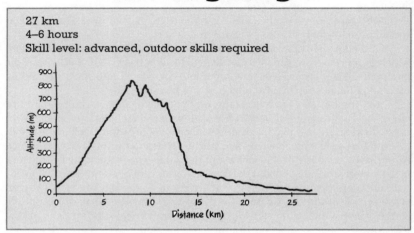

27 km
4–6 hours
Skill level: advanced, outdoor skills required

The Peaking Ridge Track is not for everyone. But for those who like really technical beech-forest single track, it's an awesome trail. If you love the start of the Wakamarina downhill with the multi-directional roots and steep, bumpy terrain this could be your new favourite ride. The track is up the top of the Richmond Ranges behind Nelson and is accessed off the top of Fringed Hill. It comes off Sunset Ridge, which in turn comes off the track running between Fringed Hill and Third House. Peaking Ridge is a recent addition to Nelson's wonderful selection of riding, thanks to the hard work of a local rider.

In the wet the tracks up here are even more challenging. As you can imagine, the off-camber slippery roots get more treacherous and the underlying surface slicker. You will certainly enjoy it more in the dry.

 **The riding**

Definitely the nicest way to start up Fringed Hill is to head up Codgers Track

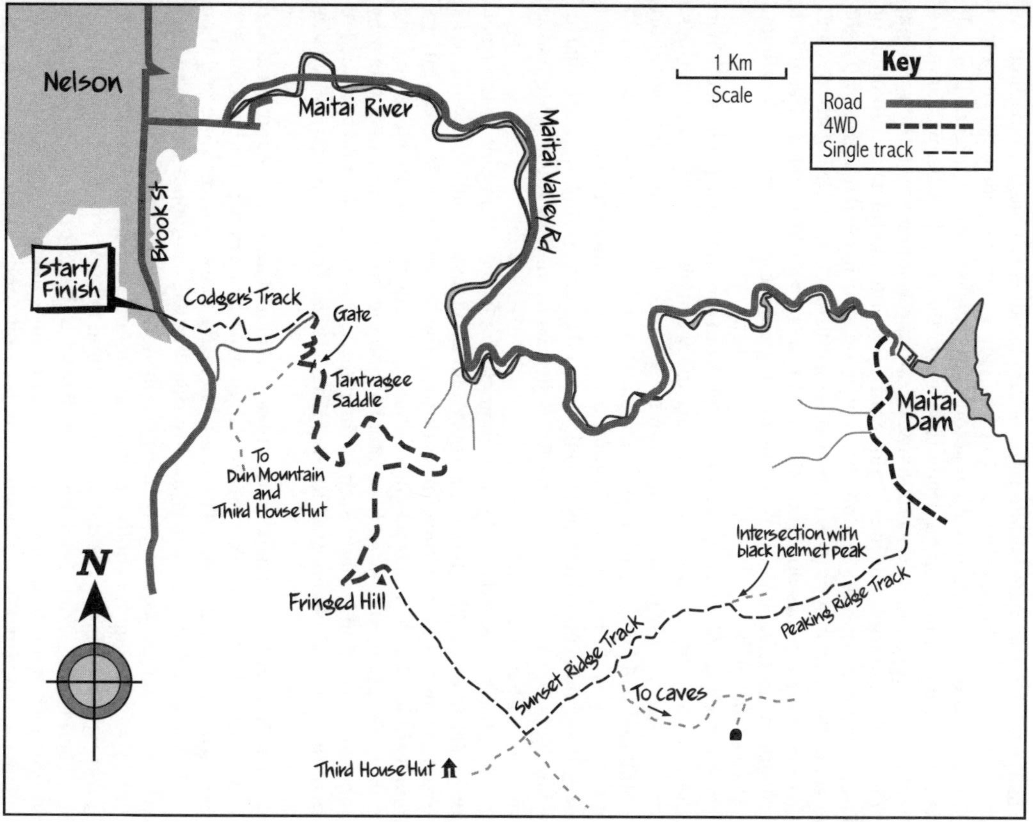

Key

Road ———
4WD – – –
Single track - - -

Scale
1 Km

Maitai Dam

Intersection with black helmet peak

Peaking Ridge Track

Smoked Ridge Track

To caves

Maitai Valley Rd

Third House Hut

Fringed Hill

Maitai River

To Dun Mountain and Third House Hut

Codger's Track

Gate

Tantragee Saddle

Brook St

Nelson

Start/Finish

N

(as for the Coppermine Saddle ride) before tackling the nasty road climb. As described above, follow Brook St up the valley, and on your left just before Blick Tce is a track marked to Dun Mountain. This becomes Codgers Track. It is 2 km of easy uphill single track that meets the road just below Tantragee Saddle. When you exit the single track continue heading up on the road and follow the sign for Tantragee Saddle rather than those for Dun Mountain or Third House. At the saddle, don't head over the stile, instead hang a sharp right around the hairpin and up the road. A short distance away is a gate to climb over. From here it is about another 5 km to the top of Fringed Hill. It is a relentless climb saved only by its bearable gradient and increasingly brilliant views of the city.

After a total of a little more than 7 km from the start is a T intersection in the road where you turn left, following the worn sign to the 'walking track' (not the car park). There is one more steep little climb before a rocky short uphill that will take you to the radio antennae on the top of Fringed Hill. Head all the way up to the top and stop for a rest at the wooden seats looking out over the wonderful view. This is well deserved after the climb of nearly 800 m. The single track you are looking for is just to the left of these seats and is marked with an arrow but no sign.

The track descends, sidles and then climbs to the high point of the track only 500 m away. The terrain is rooty and challenging but mostly rideable. From the high point the track drops through the beech forest on a very bumpy and technical track. The track then climbs again and will require some pushing before dropping down and eventually coming to a signposted four-way intersection 9.5 km from the start of the ride. At this clear junction you need to take the hard left, signposted to the Maitai Caves. This is the start of what is known as Sunset Ridge.

The Sunset Ridge Track is mostly downhill and again it is a technical and rooty single track that follows natural lines over the terrain, providing fantastic riding for advanced riders. The track is clearly marked with white and then pink tin blazes on trees. It is mostly rideable with a couple of short uphill sections that may require a push, especially if your seat is low (which it should be!). You will come to another signposted intersection at 10.9 km, where you go straight ahead towards the Maitai Dam (and not towards the caves).

The Peaking Ridge Track heads off Sunset Ridge after a total of about 11.8 km, or just under a kilometre from the previous marked intersection. It is a relatively new track and the start may be a bit tricky to find. You'll find this intersection after a few minutes of gentle uphill, which you may be walking, and past a wallow in the ground. You are waiting for the Sunset Ridge Track to pass through a cluster of four trees, which all have markers on them. A black helmet-peak is nailed on a tree just to the right and marks the top of the Peaking Ridge Track (there is a sign 20 m or so inside the top of the track). If you miss the intersection you will have to carry on up a very short but steep climb, coming out on to a dirt road. Head back a couple of hundred metres if you end up here.

The Peaking Ridge Track is all downhill, wicked root-ridden beech-forest fun. It is well marked with white marker arrows at very frequent intervals. The track is steepest at the top but mellows out considerably. It is about 2.5 km of solid technical trail that is all rideable for those with the skills. Near the end, the track enters more scrubby trees and then drops on to a dirt road.

At the dirt road you turn left and head towards the Maitai Dam. The road drops and climbs a little several times, then on a right-hand corner you will see the 'Intake Loop Walk' sign on the left. Follow this little single track for a kilometre or so as it goes over a pipe and then, as it heads uphill on farmland, drop off to the right and head towards a pedestrian bridge over the Maitai. This is about the 16 km mark. From here it is about 12 km back to town by turning left and following the gravel road and then tarseal out of the Maitai Valley. There are loads of great swimming holes in the Maitai.

 ## Coffee and food

Nelson has great food and there are plenty of opportunities for great coffee. Morrison Street Café on Hardy St is an excellent choice for coffee and food and for relaxing with the paper. Just down the road Lambretta's is a good choice too and is renowned for its pizza. There are any number of good restaurants in town, which you can wander by. Hopgoods in Trafalgar St and the Boat Shed on the waterfront both get the thumbs-up for classy cuisine. For cheap and cheerful, the kebab shop on Bridge St is a classic option.

Just out of town, The Honest Lawyer, an English country pub on Point Rd near the airport, has excellent food with a great environment. It also boasts very nice boutique hotel accommodation. A little further afield but worth the journey is The Smokehouse Café in Mapua, which has divine smoked fish to eat in or take away. On the way out there you could also check out the Mac's

Brewery in Stoke for a tour, tasting or the bar.

If you are in town on Saturday morning take a swing through the Nelson Market in Montgomery Square for local products, coffee and foodie treats.

 **Accommodation**

Like any popular town, Nelson has plenty of accommodation options. There are numerous good backpackers and motels. If you want to camp, the Maitai Valley Motor Camp is one of the best options, and the Brook Valley Motor Camp is in a good location just out of town. Avoid the Tahuna Beach Holiday Park unless you are a *Hi-De-Hi* fan.

 **Things to do**

Tahunanui Beach is Nelson's most popular swimming beach and is nice and safe, with golden sand, but often quite a few people. The Maitai River has numerous fantastic swimming holes and is my pick of places to cool off after a ride on a hot day. If you are looking for a day off riding and a nice beach then Kaiteriteri Beach near the Abel Tasman National Park is a sweet spot and the scenery out this way is fantastic.

Nelson is full of cultural and arty things to do. Visitors may be interested in the World of Wearable Art and Collectable Cars Museum near the airport. There are also numerous artists and studios you can visit, and a number of interactive workshops. The visitor information centre has the lowdown.

 **Other rides**

Nelson has plenty of other worthwhile riding opportunities. Check out the trails in the Hira Forest, off the Grampians, and other more adventurous trails in the Richmond Ranges.

> ### Contacts
> **Nelson visitor information centre**, corner Trafalgar and Halifax streets, Nelson, 03 548 2304, www.nelsonnz.com

# West Coast

The West Coast is home to stunning, rugged scenery. Its good mountain biking is separated by some reasonable distances but by considering your trip as a scenic tour as well as a bunch of great rides you can enjoy the travelling and appreciate spending time in a remote part of the country. How you string this selection of rides together depends on where you are coming from. If you are travelling from Christchurch you might like to head over Arthur's Pass and drop into Hokitika, then Blackball and pop up to Charming Creek before heading back via the Lewis Pass. If you are coming from the north it would be sensible to do things in the reverse order. If you have more time, combine this trip with the great riding in Reefton (see page 162). Any way you look at it these rides are not close together, but don't let that put you off having a great time exploring the coast and riding the best of the area's single track.

Croesus Track is a beauty, and you can round off the experience by stopping at the stunning hut. The rocky terrain makes it a bumpy challenge in parts and one that will be enjoyed by those with determination and at least intermediate technical skills. The degree of difficulty definitely goes up in the wet.

Charming Creek is a ride suitable for most mountain bikers. It is not a particularly technical ride, but the bumpiness of some rocks and old railway sleepers means you need to concentrate. Some narrow sections also provide technical challenges.

The Kaniere Water-race is easy single-track riding most of the way, interspersed with some steep staircases that require some carrying of bikes and a number of bridges to ride or walk. The drop off the left side of the track is at times steep but the track is wide enough that this is not a big issue. One potential hazard is the danger of falling into the water-race!

You'll enjoy this weekend away if you like more than moderately technical single track and appreciate fantastic scenery. But be aware that even in reasonably dry weather the tracks on the West Coast will be slippery. When it has been raining it gets worse and the rocks and roots can be treacherous.

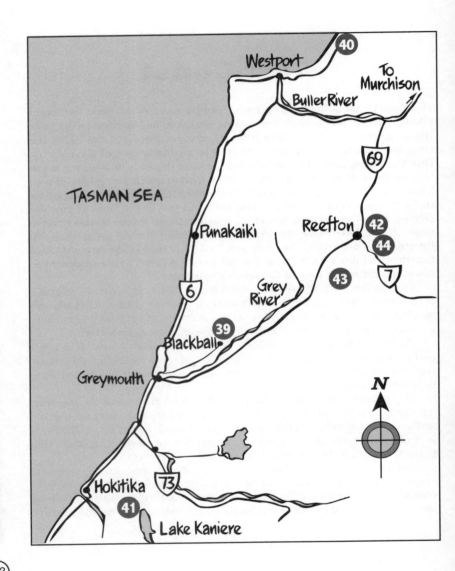

# Croesus Track

20 km return
3–6 hours
Skill level: advanced, outdoor skills required
Map: Topo K31 Blackball

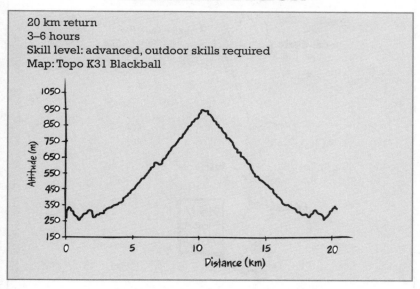

Croesus is a lovely, rocky beech-forest single track with a fascinating mining history. In many ways it is like Kirwans Track (see page 163) but provides a bumpier ride, less walking and has an easier climbing gradient. It reaches the Ces Clarke Hut, another beautiful hut with stunning views, at about 10 km. After a snack stop, or even a night here, you head back down the same way.

## The riding

Croesus Track starts 6 km out of Blackball (which is about 65 km north of Hokitika). Follow the main road through Blackball and towards Roa. About 1 km out of town, veer right, following the sign to Croesus Track. From here to

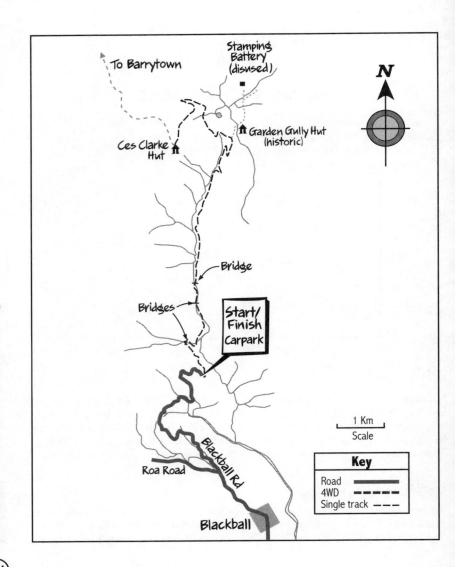

the start it is 5 km of fairly rough gravel road.

From the car-parking area the first section of track is by far the roughest but is not very long. The very bumpy rocky surface will be a challenge to most riders but don't be put off. After this initial short climb and then a flat section to recover, the track has a less rocky but still challenging descent to the first bridge, and is more readily rideable the rest of the way.

There are three swing bridges to negotiate, and these six-wire bridges can be quite a challenge with a bike. The first can be avoided by crossing in the river if the water is low but the other two will need to be tackled.

From here on the track climbs consistently but is rideable most of the way up to the huts. The track is obvious the whole way and there is little chance of getting lost. At 6.6 km there is a side track to an old mining stamping battery and the historic Garden Gully Hut (no accommodation). This is worth the diversion for interest's sake and the extra tasty bit of single track.

The Ces Clarke Hut is a beautiful 24-bunker. It is very well maintained, has water inside and a nice fire. The views into the valley from this part of the Paparoa Range are stunning.

After appreciating the hut and the views and recovering your strength, retrace your pedal strokes from this point. Obviously the track is downhill most of the way back. It is a rocky, seat-down ride on which you will appreciate your suspension. Even when the trail is completely dry, the rocks in here seem to have a slippery side they can reveal at any time. It is all good fun, except for the short uphill just before the end. The final challenge is to ride the last rock garden back to the car park.

If you are interested in a helicopter lift, Chris Cowan of Coastwide Helicopters runs a heli-bike service. Pick-up is from the Blackball Domain and he will drop you to the top, 10 or 15 minutes above the hut. You ride back to the Domain 6 km from the end of the track.

Note: For the very adventurous, epic-seeking rider there are several other riding options from here that are worth looking into if you have a topographical map. These are: continuing on the Croesus Track to Barrytown at the coast; or connecting from the Croesus Track to the Moonlight Track to form a loop. Neither is entirely rideable and you should ask around for the advice of someone who has been there recently before making an attempt as it may not increase your popularity with the friends you drag along.

# Charming Creek

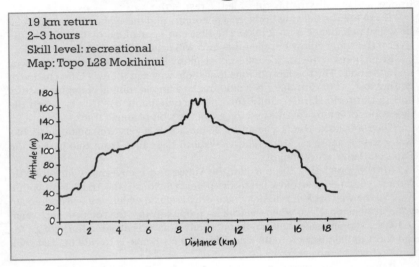

19 km return
2–3 hours
Skill level: recreational
Map: Topo L28 Mokihinui

The Charming Creek Walkway is neither a challenging nor hilly mountain-bike ride but it is worthy of inclusion for its amazing scenery through the Ngakawau River and Charming Creek gorges, and the fascinating historical relics of mining and milling days. It is a single track of varying width, at times rocky or bumpy with railway sleepers, and at times smooth and flat. It is also a great excuse to get out to the West Coast and will hopefully soon be a stop on the way to riding the Heaphy Track.

 **The riding**

You can start the Charming Creek Track from either Ngakawau or past Seddonville. Here I've described starting at the Ngakawau end, which is closer to Westport, and riding to the historic Charming Creek mine before heading back the way you came (with a slight downhill bias). The start of the track is signposted off State Highway 67 at Ngakawau. Follow the short road to the left of the mining operation and aerial ropeway, and park in the car-parking area. The start of the track is not clearly marked but is the railway-width path to the hard left of the car-parking area.

A short way along the track is a shelter with the first of many displays about the area. From here the track does not really require any navigation and is straightforward all the way to the northern end. The gradient is minimal with an overall climb of only 130 m.

The track initially follows the edge of the Ngakawau River before crossing a swing bridge and then heading up Charming Creek. The scenery is great and if it has been raining heavily (which it may well have been) the waterfalls are spectacular and the river can be very turbulent. After the swing bridge there are some rocky overhangs and some rougher short sections of track.

As the route is part of the old railway there are also sections covered with old railway sleepers, some in various states of disrepair. You will be pleased to have rear suspension here as it is pretty bumpy. The first of three tunnels is about halfway along the track — you can get away without having a torch but will probably find it easier not to ride through them as you might need the handrail!

Most of the historic mining and milling relics are on the upper part of the ride closer to the Charming Creek mine.

When the track crosses to the true left of Charming Creek there is a wide, flat section of track through grass and low bush that is not very exciting. As the track nears the mine at the upper end there is a bit more technical riding with a few unrideable obstacles and then a tunnel before it comes out at the main historic coal mine and road end. This is a good place for a break, a snack and a little exploration before heading back the same way.

The return ride is slightly downhill but this is only just noticeable. The views are completely different in this direction and you are bound to notice all sorts of things that you didn't on the way up. If you are keen on riding in this part of the country you can't help but develop a fascination with the mining history.

# Kaniere Water-race

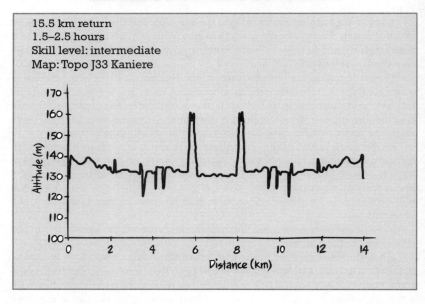

15.5 km return
1.5–2.5 hours
Skill level: intermediate
Map: Topo J33 Kaniere

The water-race track follows the channel supplying the Kaniere Forks Power Station. It is an historic track and water-race, which is still in use. The lush native bush in this area is beautiful and riding beside the almost silent flow of the water is enchanting. Overall the track has almost no gradient but has several deep ruts to cross with numerous bridged and un-bridged dry creeks.

The nicest way to ride this track is as a there-and-back ride. This maximises the single track, avoids an often muddy four-wheel drive road and any tarseal. The track is also equally good in both directions and a complete change when you look at it the other way around.

**The riding**

The start of this track is at Lake Kaniere. To get there head out of Hokitika east on Stafford St, which is off State Highway 6. Follow this as it turns into Kaniere Rd. At the settlement of Kaniere turn left into Lake Kaniere Rd, following the sign to the lake (13 km). As you reach the edge of the lake there is a T intersection where you turn left, cross a bridge over the lake outlet and then promptly park on your right. You will see the sign marking the Lake Kaniere Water-race Walkway behind you just beside the bridge on the right of the water-race.

The track enters the bush and initially runs between the water-race and the river. The first couple of kilometres are virtually all flat and smooth and very easy going. You will come out on to a dirt road that you cross straight over, continuing on. From this point the track gets a little more fun.

The next section is riddled with bridges, just about all of which are rideable. Far from detracting from the ride, the bridges are fun and don't necessarily slow you down, although some are a little challenging. There is also a number of small sets of stairs and the choice to ride or carry is sometimes yours. The rest of the track in this section is smooth and fast with winding corners and not too many technical challenges.

After a significant set of stairs, both down and then up, which have to be walked, things continue. There is a bit of a climb, then a sweet, technical, fun downhill before a wee up, at the top of which you will pop out into the open at the end of a four-wheel drive track. This point is obvious as the track continues in the open and you can see the water-race. This is a good place to have a break and then turn around and retrace your pedal strokes. If you continue from here the double track takes you down to Lake Kaniere Rd, where you can turn left and ride up the road to your car.

Lake Kaniere is a beautiful swimming lake with clear water, a reasonable temperature in the summer and lovely mountain views. Tubing the water-race is a popular activity but significant caution must be taken to avoid the tunnels it travels through.

The trail around the western side of Lake Kaniere would make a good ride for advanced riders who like technical, rooty riding and don't mind a bit of carrying along the way. This is currently only theoretical as the ride is not open to mountain bikes though this is being considered and the local mountain bike club is keen to see the track opened to bikes. If it happens it would make a

**West Coast**

riding weekend at Lake Kaniere rather lovely. Keep your ear to the ground on this one.

##  Coffee and food

There is not a lot going on in Blackball in terms of choice for food and drinks. The Formerly the Blackball Hilton pub and accommodation is the place to be for hearty meals. The Blackball store has basics and the Blackball Salami Co shop should be a stopping point if you have a taste for fantastic salami and chorizo.

Apart from the riding and the scenery, one of the best reasons to head to the West Coast near Westport is The Bayhouse Café. It is about 15 km west of Westport at Tauranga Bay and it is fantastic, with an amazing location and fantastic food and coffee. It's as stunning on a stormy day as a sunny one. If you happen to get rained out on your weekend away you could fill in a lot of time here — they do breakfast, lunch and dinner. In Westport itself, Currtino's Yellow House Café (243 Palmerston St) is probably the best bet with home-baking smells and an upbeat atmosphere. There is not a whole lot north of here and don't count on Ngakawau or Seddonville for anything.

For a small town Hokitika has a reasonable selection of food sources. Café de Paris (19 Tancred St) has good coffee and an excellent selection of food and cakes; it is also open for dinner. The Tin Shed (89 Revell St) is a decent café with a great beachfront outlook. The bakery on Revell St is also good and does takeaway pizza in the evening.

If you are heading over Arthur's Pass the Jacksons Historic Tavern at Jacksons has good food and a warm fire. The home-made pies are pretty jolly good. I have yet to find good food or coffee at Arthur's Pass Village.

##  Accommodation

The obvious and only choice in Blackball is the legendary Formerly the Blackball Hilton. It has decent double rooms and a dorm with breakfast and/or dinner included and is an experience worth having.

Westport has a lot of accommodation options though it's definitely not the highlight of the coast. There is no camping at either end of Charming Creek.

In Hokitika you can chose from a couple of backpackers and motels or something a little more upmarket. However, the pick would be to camp at the Hans Bay DOC campsite on the edge of Lake Kaniere or to look for a holiday home for rent out at the lake (ask at the information centre).

## Things to do

Swimming on the West Coast is not a common pastime — the sea tends to be pretty rugged and jolly cold. The beaches are great for a walk and the sunsets stunning. Lake Kaniere is a little treat in summertime, with swimmable water and many accessible beaches. Try Hans Bay, Lake Kaniere settlement or beaches off the Lake Kaniere Walkway.

The main activities around the West Coast are enjoying the scenery, getting out into the hills and appreciating the mining history. The coal-mining industry is still active and the not-so-scenic evidence of this can be seen around Ngakawau. More attractive to the eye is the gold-mining history of the Blackball area and all along the Croesus Track. You can arrange a guided tour of local history from the Hilton owner, and you can also explore tunnels under the town.

The West Coast's tramping and walking opportunities are too numerous to mention, but are fantastic.

### Contacts
**Coastwide Helicopters**: 03 762 6117
**Formerly the Blackball Hilton**: 26 Hart St, Blackball, 03 732 4705, www.blackballhilton.co.nz
**Westport visitor information centre**: 1 Brougham St, Westport, 03 789 6658, www.westport.org.nz
**Westland visitor information centre**: Hamilton St, Hokitika, 03 755 6166

# Reefton

The Reefton area has some of the most valuable historic relics a mountain biker could hope for — benched, perfect-gradient single tracks through beech forest. The amazing mining history of the area has left behind not only perfect riding tracks but also numerous fascinating historical sites. As you get a taste for riding in areas with such rich physical and social history, the desire to dig out more rides that explore areas such as this seems to get stronger. Visitor centres, information boards, museums and historical tours start to hold much more interest, and all this background contributes to the whole biking experience.

All three of the suggested rides in this weekend away are best suited to competent single-track riders with reasonable fitness. They all require outdoor experience as they head into fairly remote countryside where you need to be self-sufficient. In addition you need to be happy with a little bike pushing or carrying, although any effort like this will be well rewarded.

Kirwans Track is a monster uphill climb (worth every pedal stroke), followed by a sublime beech-forest single-track downhill. The hut at the top is stunning. Fit or not, many riders will enjoy the chopper-up option and the blast down. The single-track ride to Big River is a great trip and, although technical, would suit those seeking adventure and history. The Blacks Point to Waitahu Valley ride is more of an unkempt adventure for keen and skilled riders and would very nicely top off a full three or four days around Reefton.

# Kirwans Track

25 km return to hut
3–5 hours up and 1.5–3 hours down
Skill level: advanced, outdoor skills required
Map: Topo L30 Reefton

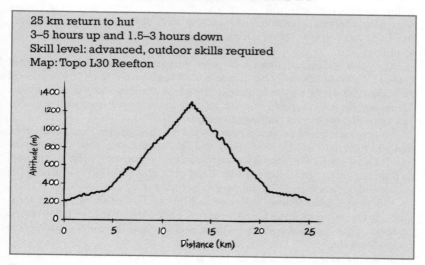

Kirwans Track is a beautiful experience, a lush beech-forest single track all the way to a stunning hut on a grassy knoll above the tree-line with amazing views. However, it is a long way up, with a solid 9 km of relentless climbing up nearly 1100 vertical metres. The uphill is mostly rideable with some fun, challenging obstacles and the downhill is, as you can imagine, fantastic.

There are several good options for this ride. If possible a night in Kirwans Hut is highly recommended because it is so lovely. You can bike up and down the track, stopping for a leisurely lunch at the hut and allowing enough time to recover for the downhill. You can bike up the track carrying minimal overnight equipment and food, stay, and bike out the next day. Or you can make the most of Airwest Helicopters' heli-bike concession and get a very reasonably priced chopper lift to the top and either stay the night and ride down the next day, or head straight down.

**The riding**

Kirwans Track starts 13 km out of Reefton. From the main part of town take State Highway 69 towards Westport/Nelson. At 10 km turn right into Boatmans Rd. A further 2 km along the road head straight where it meets gravel, and follow the sign for Capleston (which was apparently a hub of activity in mining days with 1000 residents and seven hotels). Park at the end of the road near the DOC map board. There is definitely no hotel here now, just cows and sandflies.

The track is clearly marked as it leaves the parking area. It suggests the hut is six to seven hours away but this is a very big stretch. Even if you pushed your bike the whole way most people would get there in less than five hours. There are no trail markers but the formed track is well signposted at any junctions and is obvious and easy to follow.

Shortly after the start, the track crosses a new bridge over Boatmans Creek and you turn right up the river valley and can immediately start enjoying the beech forest. At 1.7 km, after a wooden bridge, you may lose sight of the track as it ducks into a tunnel to your left. Head through the tunnel and across the swing bridge, heading left up the river valley after it.

The next 2.5 km follows the river and this section of track has the most stop-start riding, with areas that are narrow, have slipped or have fallen debris on them. There are some short carrying sections and there's some technical rooty riding too.

From about the 4 km mark the trail goes uphill pretty much all the way to the top. The gradient is easily rideable and the benched beech-forest trail is rather lovely. Apart from a few large fallen trees that DOC has kindly cut steps into and a couple of tight switchbacks you can stay on your bike most of the way. Realistically though, you will need to have plenty of breaks and recover your lungs and legs fairly frequently. If it has been raining a lot the track will be soft and heavy but still rideable.

About halfway up the hill, after a short descending section, you will pass a wider flat area on your left, which is the sight of a hotel from mining days. There are no remains but it is amazing to think of a hotel way up here.

As you get further up, the track becomes rockier and the surrounding banks are covered with moss. There may also be a little more walking as your legs get more weary.

Less than a kilometre from Kirwans Hut and just below the bush-line a track branches off to the left to an old mining hut. Continue straight ahead on the main track and shortly after this the track to the hut is marked as a turn-off to the left. Be aware that though this track is shown on topographical maps Kirwans Hut is not.

This last section of track up to Kirwans Hut is rooty and usually a bit wet and boggy. You can ride the first part but then will probably have to push another 10 or 15 minutes to the hut.

Kirwans Hut is a beauty. It is a picturesque and beautifully maintained 20-bunk DOC hut (you need an annual hut pass or hut tickets to stay here). The sights from up here are fantastic as the open ground in front of the hut affords you views of the Inangahua and Grey valleys, and surrounding hills. Apparently on a clear day you can see as far south as Mt Cook. The hut has water and a stove for heating or cooking, with coal supplied. The plush boardwalk to a toilet with a scenic view is worth a try.

If you are staying the night at Kirwans, the sunset from here can be fantastic. If you have enough energy it may be even better from the top of Kirwans Hill, which is accessible from behind the hut.

The trip down from Kirwans Hut is probably what you are waiting for and you will not be disappointed. The top section back to the signposted intersection is a challenge on the steep roots and boggy bits and many people may have to walk down here. Don't worry, the track eases up and can be enjoyed by confident intermediate-level riders from here down.

If you haven't ridden up the track you won't know what's in store. If you have you will not need to read on . . . the upper section is more rocky with some narrow trail and a few obstacles and then comes into smoother, wider beech-forest trail, a few switchbacks and a lot of lushness. The track comes parallel to the river after about 7 km at the bottom of the hill. As the track rolls along above the river there are some unrideable sections and a bit of carrying or walking is needed. Less than 2 km from the end you will cross a swing bridge, scamper through a tunnel and then eventually come out at the Boatmans Rd end, hopefully smiling widely.

The heli-biking flights are run by Alan at Airwest Helicopters. The larger your group the better the price is but the trip is pretty reasonable anyway.

# Waiuta to Big River

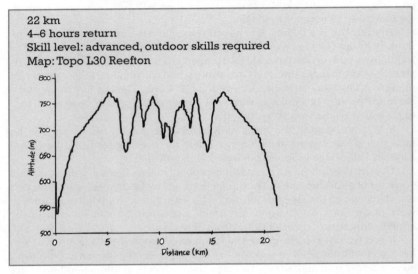

22 km
4–6 hours return
Skill level: advanced, outdoor skills required
Map: Topo L30 Reefton

The settlement of Big River is one of the most intact historic gold-mining areas left in New Zealand, and is full of fascinating relics. The DOC Big River Hut near the old settlement of Big River is a 30-bunk beauty, and one of the few back-country huts that has four-wheel drive access. There are several ways of getting to Big River and enjoying some fantastic mountain biking around this area. This description is for riding the single-track beech-forest trail from the old mining town of Waiuta to the Big River Hut and returning the way you came. The ride is technically challenging in parts and involves some bike carrying and pushing in small sections, including a couple of tricky creek crossings of deep ruts. It is suitable for keen intermediate-plus riders and people with outdoor skills, though any tricky bits can be walked, with the estimated walking time one-way being four hours.

the Mad Keen Mountain Biker's Road Trip

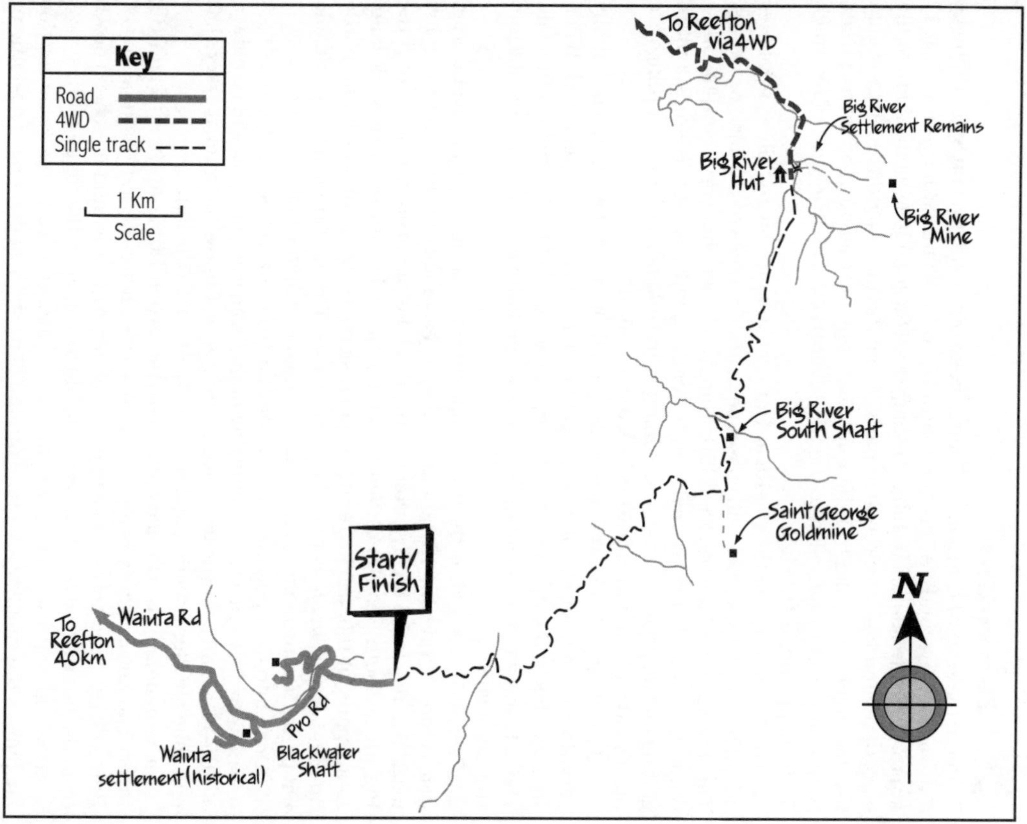

**Key**

| | |
|---|---|
| ——— | Road |
| – – – | 4WD |
| - - - | Single track |

1 Km
Scale

To Reefton via 4WD

Big River Settlement Remains

Big River Mine

Big River Hut

Big River South Shaft

Saint George Goldmine

N

Start/Finish

old Rd

Blackwater Shaft

Wairta Rd

Wairta settlement (historical)

To Reefton 40km

Reefton

**The riding**

To get to the start of the track in Waiuta, head out of Reefton on State Highway 7 towards Greymouth. After 23 km turn left onto Waiuta Rd, and follow it 17 km to the settlement of Waiuta. Parking here is a good idea as the 2 km to the start of the track is very rough in parts. From the information kiosk in Waiuta head straight ahead on Pro Rd for about 1.5 km and then turn off on to a track to the right, following a sign to the Big River track. The true start of the track is 800 m up here on the left.

The 11 km track to the Big River Hut is clear and easy to follow. It follows an old benched pack track and passes several side tracks to old mine workings. The first section of the track is a little rough and rooty but very soon smoothes out to be a wide benched track with a gentle uphill gradient. There is a bit of getting on and off to cross side streams and the odd fallen debris but things are mostly rideable and the forest is lush and beautiful.

After about 5 km of relatively easy uphill the track heads down, initially very rideable but with a short section that is in and out of a creek bed. When we rode this in the pouring rain the creek was too full to ride but is often OK. The side track to the St George's Mine is about halfway, and is a good place to stop for a snack.

Past St George's Mine the track is narrower and heads up again over terrain that is mostly rideable if you are keen and reasonably fit. At about the 8 km mark you reach the highest point of the track before dropping down past the Big River South Shaft and then pedalling up again into open tussock land. Along parts of this track are old wooden sleepers, some of which are a little off-camber and when wet can be treacherous. This section is mostly rideable but pretty bumpy in parts and has some challenging obstacles.

Once into the open land you are not far from the hut, separated only by a few boardwalks and a fun, bumpy downhill. From the track you will be able to see the river and a four-wheel drive parking area. Follow the track markers left up a quick walking section and then up the track to the hut.

It is definitely worth allowing some turnaround time at the hut and Big River. The hut is a great spot for lunch — it's sheltered and has nice views. Here you can read about some of the local mining history and then head down from the hut to have a look around the old township at the mining relics.

I would suggest you return to Waiuta just the way you came as this maximises the single-track riding around here and you don't need a shuttle or any road riding.

Another popular option is to ride to Big River over the four-wheel drive track from Soldiers Rd just out of Reefton. This is a 15 km ride through regenerating beech forest to the hut that takes two to four hours and is a more suitable option for riders looking for something less technical but still scenic and full of fascinating history. For those who have the vehicle and the know-how you could also drive in to the Big River Hut for a sweet place to stay and then bike through to Waiuta and back. Remember that if you intend to stay at the hut you need a DOC hut ticket or annual hut pass and it is worth noting that there doesn't seem to be much fuel around here for the fire.

# Blacks Point to Waitahu Valley

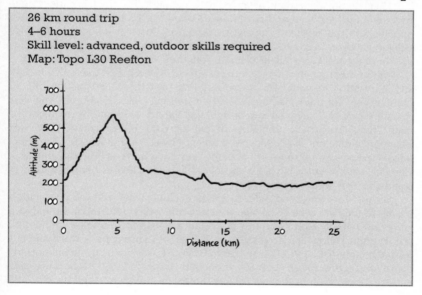

26 km round trip
4–6 hours
Skill level: advanced, outdoor skills required
Map: Topo L30 Reefton

Historic gold-mining areas and trails around Reefton again come through to provide some interesting and fun mountain biking and a bit of an adventure! The Blacks Point area has a number of trails that would potentially be very nice for riding but unfortunately DOC has tried to limit riding here by stipulating that you can ride only from Blacks Point directly to Waitahu Junction and to the Waitahu Valley.

This loop ride follows a walking track up and then a rough and in parts challenging single track down to the Waitahu River valley. A very pleasant four-wheel drive track takes you almost all the way back to Reefton, completing the loop. It's an attractive ride for those who like a bit of adventure, don't mind a little bit of bike pushing and have reasonable outdoor skills.

 ## The riding

To find the start of the ride, head out of Reefton for 2 km on State Highway 7 to Blacks Point. The Murray Creek track and parking area are obvious on your left. Head up the main track, away from the car park. The track is initially quite wide, is a nice gradient and is well maintained. Again, beautiful beech forest prevails and the surface is lovely for riding on. Apart from an up-and-down flight of stairs and a small stream crossing, it is all rideable and a very enjoyable 4.5 km to the top of the hill at Waitahu Junction.

On the way up you will pass turn-offs for the Energetic Mine on your right and Ajax Mine to your left. Keep on going past these and up the hill. At Cementown the track has been diverted around a significant slip and may require crossing a small stream and taking a short walk before rejoining the main track. The track comes more out into the open around what was Chandler's Mine and has a bit of a gradient change with a couple of ups and downs requiring a bit more effort before reaching the T of Waitahu Junction. Here the sign seems a bit older and by the look of parts of the track, they're somewhat less well maintained.

At the T junction head right on a flattish single track and follow it until it seems to almost come to an end, but actually heads left down the hill in a series of switchbacks. From this point there is very little track-marking into the Waitahu Valley. The 'tramping track' is an old mining pack track and has a great benched gradient. There is some fallen debris on the track but nothing major, and a few rough sections, especially across creeks. A bit of clearing and some attention to the low foliage that is sneaking on to the track would

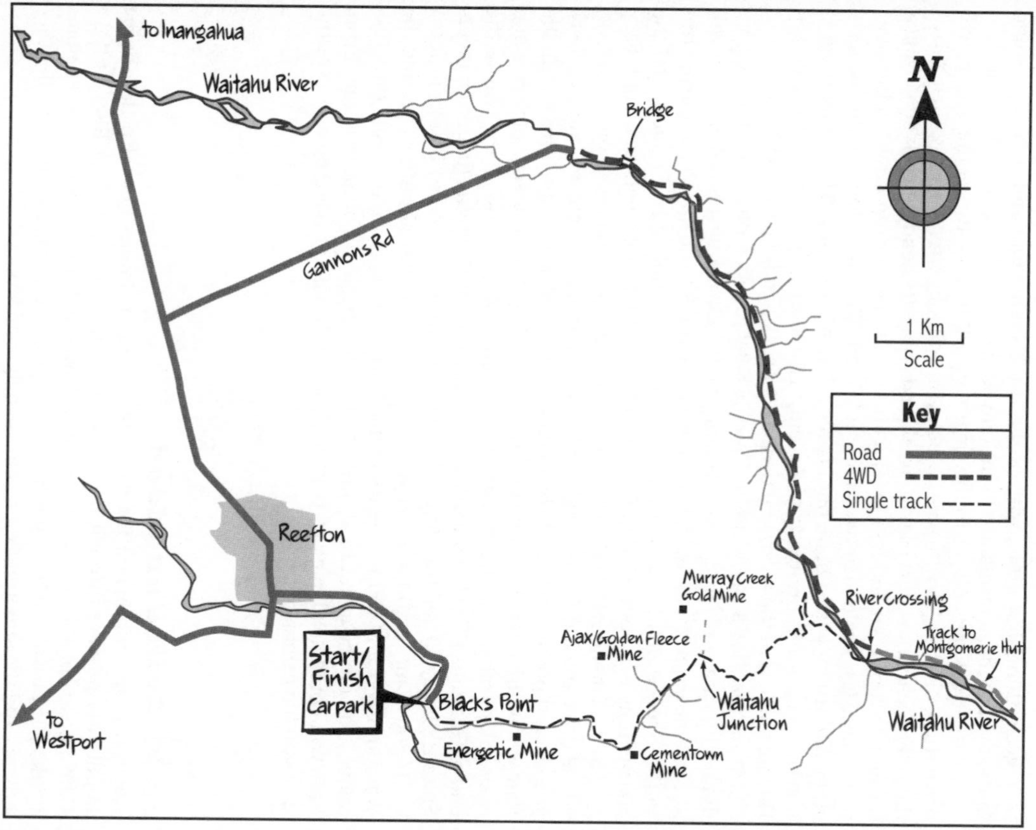

**Key**

| | |
|---|---|
| Road | ▬▬▬ |
| 4WD | ▬ ▬ ▬ |
| Single track | ▬ ▬ ▬ |

Scale — 1 Km

N

Track to Montgomerie Hut

Waitahu River

River Crossing

Bridge

Murray Creek Gold Mine

Waitahu Junction

Ajax/Golden Fleece Mine

Cementown Mine

Gannons Rd

Waitahu River

to Inangahua

Reefton

Blacks Point

Energetic Mine

Start/Finish Carpark

to Westport

be a good thing, but a majority of the track is rideable and there are some fantastic flowing sections that remind you why beech forest is the best.

As the track gets closer to the river you will be able to see the four-wheel drive track on the opposite side, which you will join after crossing. Just above the river the track seems to flatten out and continue heading upriver, getting a bit more overgrown and less clear as it goes. Look to drop down to the river near where it is braided in two at about 7.5 km. The track down to the banks is steep and tricky with a bike, but is only a few metres long. The actual track is marked with a big orange triangle only visible once you are already down! Having made it to the river, you deserve a break and this is a good place.

At normal flows the Waitahu River is easy to cross but should always be done with caution. If it has been raining and local water levels are high you will not be able to cross safely. If this is the case, expect to do an over-and-back trip to the river, which is about 15 km. This is not entirely a bad option, and the 300 m climb is an odd kind of fun if you like challenging single-track uphills.

On the far side of the riverbank head straight until you reach the main four-wheel drive track down the right of the Waitahu. Depending on exactly where you cross there may be a little bush-bashing needed. From here turn left on the four-wheel drive track and head down the valley. This is a very pleasant and easy-going track that rolls beside the river and will take you all the way to the end of Gannons Rd, 8 km outside of Reefton. Follow Gannons Rd until it meets State Highway 69 and turn left to head back to town and on to Blacks Point.

If you want to add a bit to your day you can turn right after crossing the Waitahu River and follow the four-wheel drive track in the opposite direction about 7 km up the valley to Montgomerie Hut, a basic six-bunk DOC hut. From here you could head back as per the described route or back up and over the way you have come.

 **Coffee and food**

Reefton is not renowned for its culinary opportunities but with the tourist population passing through has some reasonable options. The Reef Cottage Café does probably the best coffee in town and a good selection of home cooking. Clarisa's Café on the way out of town to Kirwans does excellent ice creams and the supermarket is surprisingly well stocked.

**Accommodation**

Reefton has a reasonable selection of accommodation from motels to B&Bs and a local camping ground. However, an overnight riding trip to Big River or Kirwans Hut should definitely be considered. There are also camping spots near the start of Kirwans and at Waiuta. The DOC-owned historic Waiuta Lodge is worth investigating as a base and can sleep 30.

 **Things to do**

There are a lot of tramping and walking opportunities around the Reefton area but as many of them are also bikeable you are better off pedalling. The visitor centre also has a brochure on the Victoria Conservation Park that describes all the walks in the area.

If you fancy a swim, you should be able to find a good spot in the Inangahua River. If you have a four-wheel drive you can venture out to the Big River and Montgomerie huts, either for accommodation, adventure or as a ride starting point.

The mining history of this area is fascinating and it is great to be able to combine such intriguing relics and social history with biking. Gold mining brought Reefton to life in the 1870s and numerous buildings from this era still exist and are worth a wander around, as is the Blacks Point museum. The Reefton Heritage Walk takes in the best of these remains. Reefton also prides itself on generating the first public supply of electricity and being the first town to have electric streetlights.

The Reefton Goldfields area has numerous historic mining sites, including those around Kirwans Track, Waiuta, Big River and Blacks Point.

---

### Contacts

**DOC office and Reefton visitor information centre**:
67 Broadway, Reefton, 03 732 8391, www.reefton.co.nz
**Airwest Helicopters**: 03 732 8882

# Hanmer Springs

**Hanmer Springs is 130 km north of Christchurch in North Canterbury. The town prides itself on being a unique alpine spa village and the largest thermal resort in the South Island. As well as its other recreational activities, Hanmer is becoming an increasingly popular mountain-biking destination.**

The mountain-biking trails around Hanmer cater to a diverse range of abilities and will provide enjoyment for family and recreational riders as well as those with more skill.

Hanmer is the perfect destination for a relaxed weekend away, and it is especially suitable for families and groups. It is a very small town that is well focused on catering to visitors. The village has a variety of accommodation, cafés and restaurants and everything is within walking distance.

The fantastic natural thermal pools are the attraction that Hanmer is best known for. This adds a whole other element of rest and recreation to a weekend away, either for relaxing post-ride legs or just whiling away the hours. Both summer and winter these fantastic pools are a major drawcard.

You could dash to Hanmer for a day's riding from Christchurch but you would be missing the point of a visit, which is as much about slowing down and chilling out as the fine single-track riding on offer.

# Hanmer Sweet Single Track

2–3 hours of single-track riding and exploring
Skill level: recreational/intermediate
Map: Hanmer Springs Mountain Bike Track Guide

The Hanmer Forest is where the biking's at. It's a privately owned working forest managed by Matariki Forests. The Heritage Forest area, to the south of Jollies Pass Rd, is a covenanted recreational area that has many old-growth trees and a diverse collection of exotic species.

The Hanmer Springs Mountain Bike Club constructs and maintains all the purpose-built mountain-bike tracks in the forest. The club produces a map of the tracks, which is available from the information office and the Wild Life clothing store in the main street. This map is an invaluable resource and is a must for all first-timers to the area. Proceeds from the sale of the map go into trail development and maintenance.

As it's a commercial forest, access to the area is reliant on the goodwill and continuing excellent relationship with the forest owners. The ever-changing nature of trails is a consequence of the logging and regrowth of trees in the area and this makes it tricky to provide a definitive trail guide. Nice as it would be to provide a planned route through the best single track, this is not possible so the following is an overview of the riding here and what to expect. When combined with the most up-to-date map and a little scouting around, it should help you find most of the sweet trails.

The area containing the mountain-bike tracks in Hanmer is bordered by the Chatterton River to the west, Jollies Pass Rd to the south and DOC land to the north-east.

The easiest way to get into the trails is to head out of town on Jollies Pass Rd. After crossing Dog Stream and heading up the hill past the DOC office turn left into Pawsons Rd and a couple of hundred metres up here you will find the Dog Stream Track on your right. This is a shared-use single track that leads up into the forest and gets you started on some fine riding if you choose to ride it over the Jolliffe Saddle Track.

Most of the mountain-bike trails in the Hanmer Forest are hand made and purpose-built. They use the natural terrain and gradient well and flow with nicely shaped corners, weaving through the trees. There are plenty of fun sections of trail that you will happily ride again and again. Most of the trails are under the cover of the forest, except where they have been rebuilt in regenerating pines. Although a large majority of the riding is in exotic pine there is a tasty little offering of natives as well.

The trail development here is fluid; as new trails are built others slip away into the harvesting cycle. The Hanmer Mountain Bike Club is involved in ongoing trail development and assures me that there will always be good single track here, and hopes to keep the rate of growth greater than the rate of loss to the forestry. During the researching of this book, two trails have been logged over but three new trails have been introduced.

The heritage area of the forest is an easy non-technical ride during the day and a popular night-riding spot worth cruising through if you have lights.

Note: Remember that this area is a working forest and you need to obey normal road rules, beware of forestry vehicles using the roads, obey all forest-management signs and only ride on designated mountain-bike trails and roads.

# **Family Riding**

10 km of roads and trails
Skill level: recreational
Map: Hanmer Springs Mountain Bike Track Guide

The flat, wider tracks to the south of Jollies Pass Rd in the area known as the Heritage Forest provide ideal terrain for beginners and family groups. These tracks can be approached from town at the end of Bath St, or off Jollies Pass Rd on the right after you have crossed over Dog Stream.

The tracks are in a protected mature plantation with many different species of pine trees. Thanks to the local club the tracks have had a lot of gravelling over recent years, meaning you can happily ride here in the wet. Alligator Alley is the exception to this, a great mud plug on someone else's bike! This part of the forest is virtually flat with a mixture of mountain-bike specific single-track and forest roads. It is a great spot to warm up or down before tackling the harder trails or to do with the family.

 ## Coffee and food

Local recommendations include the Springs Deli Café, which is consistently good and has dramatically improved its coffee. The Log Cabin is a classic Kiwi diner and Hanmer institution; it opens early (7am) and closes late (10pm). Try the blue cod and chips. Most people miss the Garden House Café as it is in the pools complex. It is a good spot if friends are in the pools and you're not, as you don't need a pool pass to enter the café. The Hanmer Springs Bakery has excellent post-ride afghan biscuits! Hot Springs Bar and Bistro has very good value meals with heaps of space for a large group. The ½ Roast is a local favourite.

 ## Accommodation

Accommodation in Hanmer is very affordable with a large variety of motels, campgrounds, holiday homes and B&Bs. One of the most attractive options is the prolific and easily accessible number of holiday homes for rent.

Here are a few suggestions: the Alpine Adventure Tourist Park is at the end of Jacks Pass Rd and is nice and quiet. Hanmer Springs Forest Camp, 4 km out of the village up Jollies Pass Rd, has camping and a good range of cabins, with biking at your tent door. Alpine Holiday Apartments and Campground, also on Jollies Pass Rd, is a good spot if Hanmer is busy as not many people know about it. Drifters Inn provides lodge accommodation and is a real find for a large group, with a communal kitchen, BBQ and dining area. The cosy schist open fire is great on a cold night.

As mentioned, the rental of private holiday homes in Hanmer is big business. This is a fantastic option with all the comforts of home, plenty of space and very reasonable prices. Two organisations are responsible for most of this — Hanmer Holiday Homes (www.hanmerholidayhomes.co.nz) and Kiwi Escapes Holiday Homes (www.kiwiescapes.com).

**Things to do**

Hanmer Springs Thermal Pools and Spa has a selection of mineral pools, private pools, freshwater pools, separate kids' pools and a hydroslide. They also have massage and pamper packages (it pays to book in advance through the visitor centre) if you want to treat yourself.

The Clarence River heading into the Molesworth (over Jacks or Jollies Pass) offers good swimming options that you can ride or drive to in the summer months.

There are plenty of walking opportunities around Hanmer. The information centre has the Hanmer Forest Recreation Map with descriptions of all the walks, from very short to whole-day efforts.

Hanmer also has a picturesque 18-hole golf course in town.

> ## Contacts
> **Hurunui visitor information centre**: next to the pools, Hanmer, 03 315 7128.

# Canterbury

**Canterbury has some fantastic mountain biking. From the narrow and flowing Port Hills tracks so close to the city, to the lush beech forest in the foothills of the Southern Alps, there is plenty of sweet single track to be had.**

This long weekend of biking out of Christchurch is a tasting platter of the types of riding available. It is not the only riding by a very long way, but rather a selection of the not-to-be-missed rides.

If you're a visitor to Christchurch, this is a great opportunity to get a perspective on the city from above and to get into the stunning scenery of the hills towards Arthur's Pass.

The Port Hills tracks are predominantly in open terrain; they are narrow with fun rocky challenges and the views are fantastic. The tracks are suitable for confident mountain bikers but will be enjoyed at slower speeds by keen riders from recreational level up. It is reasonably hard to get lost in the Port Hills but you can get pretty tired! Keep an eye out for the guy repairing his home built on the side of these trails.

The Wharfedale Track is a classic day out from Christchurch. It is great, easy-going single track with some moderately technical challenges, suitable for intermediate-level riders and above. There are options for a point-to-point ride, a there-and-back option, an overnight stay in a hut or contemplating one of the bigger rides in this area, Black Hill or Mt Oxford.

Craigieburn is beautiful beech single track with fantastic scenery. The riding here is typical of beech forest — rooty and moderately to very technical. Several sections of track cross scree slopes, which makes for some psychologically challenging riding. This ride is suitable for confident intermediate and more advanced riders.

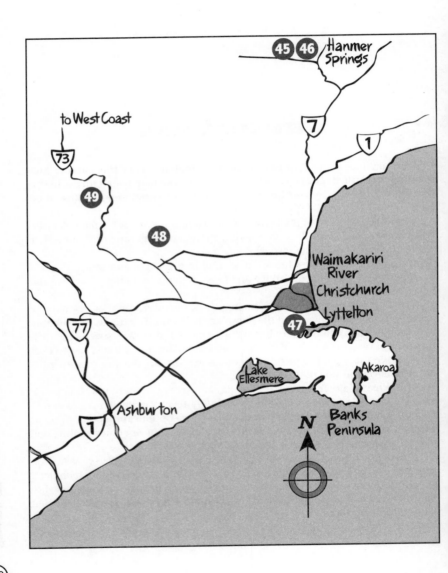

# Port Hills

> Up to 40 km of trails
> Map: Port Hills mountain-biking map

Christchurch has a mass of riding close to the city on the Port Hills. The hills are covered with purpose-built mountain-biking tracks, walking and shared-use tracks. The ultimate aim of a complete riding traverse of the hills is getting close. The Port Hills run west to east, south of Christchurch city. They are close enough to town that you don't really need a car to get to them, and many locals ride from their doorsteps. The hills are mostly open and covered in grass, tussock, rocks and sometimes cloud. A couple of areas such as Victoria Park have dense exotic forest, which makes a nice riding change. In the summer things can be very hot and exposed; conversely, when the wind is up and temperature down, it can be super chilly up there. Winter night riding can be a very rewarding experience.

Christchurch City Council has produced a *Port Hills Mountain Biking* brochure, which has a good map and some track information. You can download it from www.ccc.govt.nz or the Ground Effect website, www.groundeffect.co.nz.

The two loops described below cover some of the best trails and will give you a good introduction and orientation to the area for a day of riding, but there is plenty more. At the western end of the Port Hills there are a number of riding options that go either up or down the valleys. There is also a traversing track near Summit Rd that almost spans the whole of the Port Hills.

## Captain Thomas to Anaconda

> 22 km
> 1.5–3 hours
> Skill level: intermediate

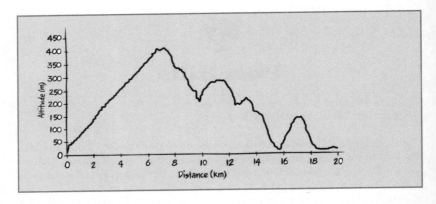

This loop is at the eastern end of the Port Hills, starting from Sumner and eventually returning via Taylors Mistake. Sumner is a great place to start from because you will end the ride with a descent from any direction. It is also a fantastic place for a café or swim stop before or after your ride. The track contains some great single track and the views are some of the best on the Port Hills.

 **The riding**

The Captain Thomas Track leads from Sumner to Evans Pass, starting at Wakefield Reserve, on Wakefield Ave in Sumner. The track is about 500 m from the Sumner shops on the right. It is a very pleasant climb of 3 km up a narrow single track with a very nice gradient. There are a few obstacles to walk that are signposted from the other direction as technical challenges. This is a shared-use track and can be quite busy.

As you get closer to Evans Pass (which you will be able to see), veer right following the bike signs to stay on the track until it comes out on Summit Rd just above the pass. Turn right here and follow the road as it winds gently up for nearly 4 km.

At the second sign for Greenwood Park on your left, on a right-hand bend in the road, you will see a mountain-bike track sign as well. This is the track you are looking for. It heads away from the road in the direction you have come from and is 4 km of fun, flowing single track back to Evans Pass. It is possible to visit the gun emplacements by turning right when you cross a farm road at the end of the uphill (on the single track). A cheeky but tricky trail also exits to Lyttelton from there.

Back at Evans Pass, turn right back on to the Summit Rd, (riding past where you came up earlier), head straight ahead towards Godley Head (the most dodgy intersection in Christchurch) and just over the cattle-stop hang a sharp right into the mountain-bike track. This is signposted here as Scarborough Hill Reserve and the Crater Rim Walkway. This track is 4.5 km of rolling fun single track to Breeze Col, where you will see a map board on the opposite side of the road. This is where the last sweet section of single track to Taylors Mistake Beach starts from.

Follow the sign directing you to this fantastic little beach. The top part of the track is shared use but you will soon see a sign to Anaconda mountain-bike track directing you left. Just follow this all-downhill trail right to the beach car park. It is fast and flowing and a real blast.

The very bottom section (shared use again) is popular with walkers so be careful. When you get to the beach car park head up the only road out of there.

To get back to where you started, climb on the tarseal to the top of the hill. When the road turns left into Scarborough Rd, go straight ahead into a car park and follow the Scarborough Park Loop track down the hill. This is a cheeky little shortcut to make the most of the stunning views over Sumner. When the track comes out above the sea turn left and head downhill. At the first intersection head straight and then right into Nayland St. Follow this all the way to Stoke St, where you turn left and then come out on to Wakefield Ave again.

Note: The Captain Thomas Track is a great downhill, and if you can work out a shuttle, is well worth riding down.

## Rapaki Track to Victoria Park

14 km
1–2 hours
Skill level: intermediate

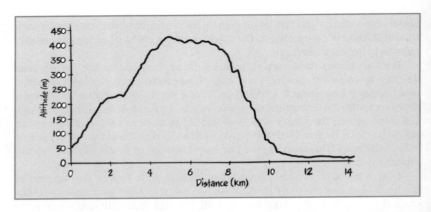

The ride up the Rapaki Track and down through Victoria Park is a classic short Port Hills loop with an easyish climb, some great single-track traversing and a technical blast down through Victoria Park with a number of track options.

The Rapaki Track starts at the end of Rapaki Rd in St Martins. There is car parking here if you are driving. Head up the four-wheel drive track, which you follow for nearly 4 km to where it meets Summit Rd. This is non-technical riding but it is a reasonable climb.

At Summit Rd veer right and head straight into the Mt Vernon Track (shared use) on the opposite side of the road. This is a nice single track that climbs slowly with undulations for a kilometre or so, providing great views. The track has a couple of switchbacks (up) and then drops a little more steeply to reach the road 5.1 km from the start of the ride. The next piece of track is on the opposite side of the road, starting at the gate you can see. Roll on, past Lava Flows on your right (if you wish, you could head down here — it is steepish, with some rocks).

Arriving at the pines will place you at the top of Victoria Park. Putting your seat down here isn't a bad idea. From here you should head straight/veer right, which will take you through a nice little bit of forest and out the ridge. Roll down the ridge (over the 'sheep stop') and into a rockier section. You should hit the Victoria Park jump park with a new series of gaps on your left.

From here head down any way you wish; keeping to the right will help you avoid the main road and walking-only trails. A reasonable way down is to head right and up a little on the major dirt road, then along until you find a hub of trails with a massive jump on your right (uphill). Turn left here, then a couple of metres down veer right into a trail with some obstacles (with chicken lines around them you can take). From here, cross the road, head down, at the end turn left (on the road), then quick right across the small bridge and out into the open. Keep on riding and you'll come to another small bridge — turn left, then go straight ahead, down, and into the forest again. This track ends with a steep clay bank into the bottom of the valley, roll out, watch out for magpies and cross the locked gate at the end of the trail, exiting on to the tarseal.

To get back to your car, follow the sealed road (Bowenvale Tce) to the end. Turn right on to Centaurus Rd, then follow Centaurus as it hangs a sharp right (tricky) around the bottom of the hills. At the roundabout, get yourself on to Port Hills Rd (straight) and then right on to Rapaki Rd.

# Wharfedale

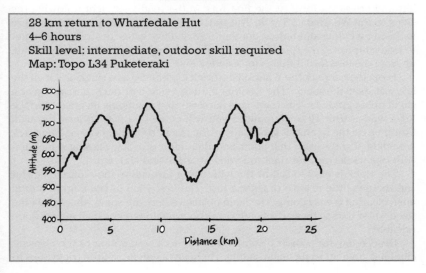

28 km return to Wharfedale Hut
4–6 hours
Skill level: intermediate, outdoor skill required
Map: Topo L34 Puketeraki

The Wharfedale track is lovely, a fine, native-bush clad single track for 14 km to a hut and an equally enjoyable return trip. The riding is moderately technical, with a few more difficult sections requiring some getting on and off. The gradient is very pleasant the whole way. Don't be tempted to do a one-way trip as the single-track return is much nicer than a ride out the farm road, and the time taken for a car shuttle could be much better spent at the local café. Any thought of riding a complete loop back to the car on the road should be considered at your peril — it sounds crazy to me! The nicest options are to ride into the Wharfedale Hut and back as described here or, for a shorter ride, to the saddle and back (18 km return).

 **The riding**

The start of the Wharfedale Track is 20 km from Oxford (55 km north-west of Christchurch). Follow the main street through Oxford heading south-west. After 3 km turn right into Woodstock Rd (signposted to View Hill). Follow this for nearly 10 km before turning right into Ingrams Rd (gravel). There may or may not be a road sign here. About 400 m along, the road does a 90-degree turn left and crosses a ford. At the first fork in the road veer right following the signs to the Wharfedale Track. The start of the track is signposted from here and is six winding kilometres, another ford and five gates away. Be careful not to lose your car in the ford if there has been a lot of rain. You may want to ride up from the first ford if things look dodgy.

From the car park the Wharfedale Track leads away as a single track on the left just over the fence. The track is initially wide and fairly flat with just a slight uphill gradient. The track gets narrower but maintains its gravel surface for a while. After 10 to 15 minutes you will come to a gate to pass through. Continue on the main track, passing by the track to Coopers Creek. The track descends slightly from this point and then climbs again, passing a junction with two tracks on your right to Rydes Waterfall and Mt Oxford.

The track is easy to follow the whole way through to the Wharfedale Hut and there is little chance of getting lost. The first 4 km of track up to a little open clearing is easy going. The main obstacles here are some wheel-grabbing sized water bars to be wary of and a few rooty sections, almost all of which are rideable.

Descending for a short distance will lead to a resumption of the pleasant climbing gradient to the main saddle. There are a couple of little tricky dips to cross along here and a few wee obstacles but nothing major, all very pleasant. If the weather has been inclement and wintry this area might have a bit of snow — the track will occasionally have a white dusting on the trees or ice on the ground. Although it is not the most perfect time to ride the track, it can add to the adventure, but be dressed for it!

The main saddle is at about 9 km and it's obvious. It has signs in both directions and nice sitting spots for morning tea. This is the place to turn around if you want to head back rather than onward to the hut.

From the saddle it is only 30 to 50 minutes down to the hut. It is all lovely lush single track that winds its way down through the forest. There are a couple of tricky deep dips in the track and a couple of stream crossings. At nearly 14 km you will come to a river crossing where you might get your feet wet, and a ladder of wooden steps. The hut is just around the corner.

The Wharfedale Hut is an eight-bunk DOC hut with a log fire and toilet but no running water (try the stream nearby). It is a nice place to spend the night especially if you are tempted to do any other exploring in the area. From the hut you follow the track back the way you came, up to the main saddle and then just about all downhill back to your car.

Other options for keen and experienced technical riders (and those who don't mind a bit of walking) include heading down from the Wharfedale Hut to the old Townsend Hut site and up the track towards Blackhill Hut before completing the loop back on to the Wharfedale Track, which joins the track midway up the climb to the saddle. There is a decent uphill push in here that can be a little overgrown, but there is also some very worthwhile riding.

The loop via Mt Oxford from the Coopers Creek end is a fantastic option if you are not put off by a solid 1.5-hour uphill carry to the top. The track then runs along the ridge with some tricky technical riding on the tops and into amazing old forest. The track drops down on to the Wharfedale where you head back towards the start before hanging a left back down the Coopers Creek Track. For both the above suggestions, refer to the appropriate topo map.

As an added extra option, slightly more technical than the Wharfedale, the Coopers Creek Track is a sweet little trail that heads downhill from the gate less than a kilometre from the start. If you can talk someone into picking you up from the end of it, it is a great addition to the ride. The track comes out at the end of Mountain Rd, which is a continuation of Mounseys Rd, signposted off Woodstock Rd. The track is damp, thus making summer a better time to ride.

# Craigieburn

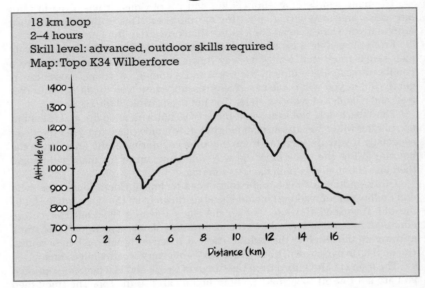

18 km loop
2–4 hours
Skill level: advanced, outdoor skills required
Map: Topo K34 Wilberforce

The Craigieburn Forest Park has some amazing riding opportunities. The most popular riding in here is on the lovely trails around the Craigieburn Valley recreational area. These tracks are more suited to intermediate and advanced technical riders due to the off-camber trail, exposed nature and rooty beech forest. The trails here are best in the dry but can be enjoyed when a little more slippery also. Bear in mind that being in the alpine area they are usually closed by snow in the winter and that even in fine weather it can be jolly cold.

Described here is a figure-eight loop ride that starts in the Broken River ski field valley, cutting across to the Craigieburn ski field valley before returning to where you started. You can also start this ride by heading directly up the Craigieburn ski field road to 'The Edge' track.

**The riding**

To get to the Craigieburn area trails follow State Highway 73 west out of Christchurch for about 100 km. After passing the Castle Hill settlement, look out for the sign to Broken River Skifield/Craigieburn Valley recreation area on your left. Just inside the gate is a day shelter with a toilet and car parking. This is where you start from.

From your car head up the gravel road for only a matter of metres before heading off to the right, cross the creek on the bridge and head on to a single track marked to Lyndon Saddle. It is only 1.5 km to the saddle from here but it feels deceptively long. The single track climbs up through native beech forest with roots to contend with and some short sections of challenging gradient but it is all rideable, bar one tricky corner (up only).

When the track comes out to a small clearing at a four-way intersection you have reached Lyndon Saddle, a nice place for a short stop. From here you want to take the option that goes over the saddle into the next valley to your right. It may be marked 'Craigieburn Valley 15 mins'. From here the track descends (seat down) through a more open section before coming to an intersection. Here you want to turn hard right following the 'Skifield road 15 mins' sign, and gobble up the lush single track on offer.

When the track comes out to the road 4.3 km from the start (this is the Craigieburn ski field road), turn left and head up the gravel. It is about 5 km up this road to the bottom of the ski area. It is a pleasant-gradient climb so just enjoy the scenery. You will pass a gate that is usually closed and locked in summer and then, as you get higher, two ends of a marked foot track on your left. Pass by the ski field car park — keeping on the road (right) leading up. This will take you past the ski field ticket office and toilets; head towards the tow — straight/left — and after passing under the lower end of a rope tow look straight ahead to see a narrow single track across the scree slope. This is where you are headed. The track is not signposted but known as 'The Edge' for reasons that will become obvious.

This part of the track provides the trickiest riding in the loop. Traversing the scree slopes can be nerve-wracking as it is narrow and a little unstable and on the side of a very steep hill. It is not a crime to walk if your confidence betrays you. When the track re-enters the bush it is still narrow in parts and has some tricky little sections for experienced riders. At nearly 12 km from the start you will return to an intersection you were at previously. Head right here, uphill, and you will shortly be back at the Lyndon Saddle intersection. (For those who have been here before, the track was tidied up in 2007 — thus making it possible to ride the entire trail without getting off.)

A cheeky little side trip from Lyndon Saddle is to ride/push up the track to Helicopter Hill (the only track going up from here) and enjoy the fun rooty ride back down.

From the saddle head down on the track marked 'Visitor Centre 75 mins'. This is known as 'The Luge'. It's a rollicking jaunt down the hill on typical rooty beech-forest trail. You can't help but love it and will probably want to do it again and again. This trail comes out on to the Broken River ski field road about 2 km above where you parked your car. Turn left to head back down there. The Luge also makes a very nice uphill, which you could use instead of the other uphill track if you fancy less of a gradient.

The other popular piece of track in this area is the track to Dracophyllum Flat. It is probably best done added on to this ride as a there-and-back effort. To do this, turn right out of the bottom of The Luge and head up the hill on the gravel road. Follow the gravel to the top of the hill until a T intersection with another gravel road coming in from the left and look out for a single track heading straight on the far side of the road. Head into the track downhill; it is lush beech-forest riding and great fun. Cross the river at the bottom then head up the other side. The track undulates for a while before coming out into an open area. From here the track can be a little more tricky as it passes through another two or three open areas with the actual marked trail less clearly defined. Keep an eye out for markers and if you can't see them or any track marks head back until you can. The track then ducks back into the bush and climbs up before coming out within sight of Forest Lodge. At this point make sure you stay right and don't be tempted to take a shortcut left and out into the tussock — this is lumpy land! From Forest Lodge you can return the way you came or head down the Mt Cheeseman ski field road and back out to the main highway, turn left and go back towards Broken River.

There is a lot of other exploring to do in the Craigieburn Forest Park. Keen technical riders looking for a challenge could consider the two-day trip around the Cass-Lagoon loop with a stop at Hamilton Hut or a short jaunt up and back on the Lagoon Saddle track. The Cass Saddle track would be a fun up-and-back if it weren't for the riverbed riding. Scree riding from the Broken River/Camp Saddle down to The Edge trail is another keen bean thing to do — for the brave only.

**Coffee and food**

In a city the size of Christchurch it's hard to pick just a few. However, Sumner is a popular spot in summer and is a good stop before heading up the Captain Thomas Track. Lyttelton has a number of good cafés but riding up the Bridal Path is an evil experience and is the only off-road route up so it's better you come by car.

Outside of the city you can't go past celebrity chef Jo Seagar's café in Oxford (78 Main St) for hearty pre-ride breakfasts and coffee.

If you are heading to Craigieburn you may like to be able to pass comment on the Sheffield Pie Shop versus Springfield pies rivalry. In Springfield, the pies are at the café second on the right as you pass through town. Try asking for sauce and see what reaction you get.

 **Accommodation**

Christchurch has all types of accommodation, as you'd expect in a city of its size. There is no recommendable local camping but the Craigieburn Valley recreation area has basic DOC camping near the start of the ride there with lovely mountain views. There are a number of other places up near here where you can also camp.

 **Things to do**

In the summer you can swim and surf at Sumner, Taylors Mistake and the beaches near New Brighton/South Shore or relax at Cass Bay on Lyttelton Harbour. The Port Hills have some excellent climbing close to the city and Castle Hill on the way to Craigieburn is a bouldering paradise.

The hills around the Craigieburn area and right through the Canterbury foothills have amazing tramping opportunities from a few hours to days. The DOC offices in Christchurch and Arthur's Pass have loads of information.

Christchurch is full of potential for cultural activities. The new contemporary art gallery is full of great stuff. The Arts Centre has galleries and shops. There is theatre, opera and general city stuff. Many people enjoy a trip to Lyttelton for the relaxed main street café scene.

**Other rides**

There is a lot more riding to do in the Port Hills around Christchurch. For easier single track try the mountain bike trails at Bottle Lake and McLeans Island. For much more advanced and challenging trails check out Mt Oxford, Mt Richardson, Mt Thomas or Mt Grey.

**Contacts**
**Christchurch visitor information centre**: Cathedral Square, 03 379 9629, www.christchurchnz.net

# Queenstown

**Queenstown has a proliferation of fantastic mountain-bike riding and some of the country's most stunning scenery. It has a proactive mountain-biking community and is sprouting new trails and venues all over the place. It is also a highly popular destination filled with tourists, shopping and expensive adrenalin activities, most of which the do-it-yourself Kiwi mountain-bike rider can do without. However, this does mean there are plenty of options for dining out, cruising the town, seeing the sights and a bit of nightlife if that is your thing.**

This selection of Queenstown rides is a taster that would keep you pretty busy for a long weekend but is by no means a complete collection. The Moonlight and Moke Lake tracks are a classic Queenstown cross-country ride, modified here to maximise the single track and minimise the faff factor. It is a decent day out for fit riders with a lot of sweet single track, technical in a few parts, and the scenery is stunning. The new trail development at Seven Mile Point was still under construction at the time of writing. However, considering the existing trails, the proposal and the track record of the trail builders it is guaranteed to be great. There will eventually be 20–25 km of specially crafted XC-style single track with options for all levels. For some really fun technical single track the Fernhill Loop track and Vertigo are also Queenstown classics — you need to be happy with riding uphill, not mind a little bit of pushing and be hanging out for a challenging rooty descent.

The Pack Track into Skippers Canyon is included for a short treat, something you could shuttle that would be enjoyed by most riders and could be tied up with a ride at Coronet Peak in the summer. For jumping and skills the Gorge Road Jump Park and Wynyard Terrain Park are where it's at, or you can just watch others doing what you wish you could.

A basic trail map on Queenstown is available from local bike shops.

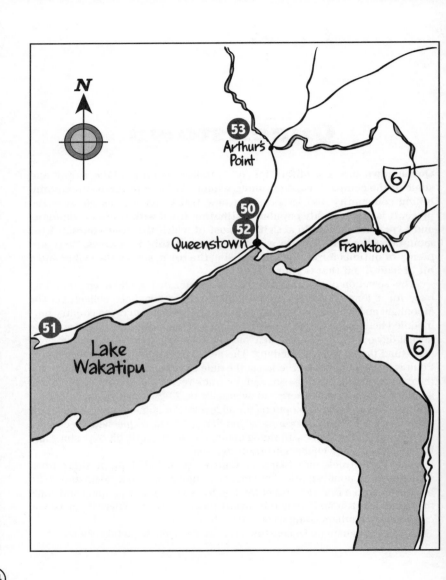

# Moonlight and Moke Lake

31 km
4–6 hours
Skill level: intermediate
Map: Topo E41 Queenstown, Queenstown Mountain Bike Trails map

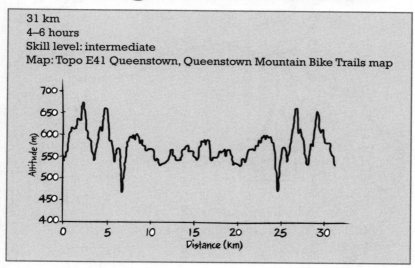

The Moonlight and Moke Lake tracks are the epitome of classic Queenstown cross-country riding. The Shotover River and the Moonlight and Moke creeks and surrounding countryside provide superb views. The trail is a mix of fun, technical single track, rolling (sometimes steep) four-wheel drive road and beautiful single track around the lake. There are several ways you could make a day of this ride, but this option maximises the single track and eliminates the need for road riding or shuttles. This 'lollipop' loop takes in the Moonlight Track, the road to Moke Lake, loops around the lake and returns the way you have come via the Moonlight Track.

The Moonlight Track passes through the Ben Lomond Station, which is private property so make sure you leave gates as you find them and try not to be too peeved by the cowpats and the mess they make.

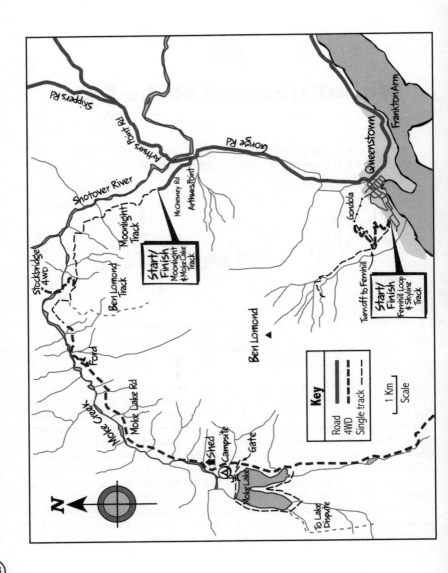

**The riding**

To get to the start of the Moonlight Track head out of Queenstown on Gorge Rd to Arthur's Point. Just after the pub turn left onto McChesney Rd and head up the hill, following this road and the Moonlight Track signs to a parking area.

From the car park follow the road ahead for a very short distance before heading off on to the obvious single track on your left (which should be signposted as the Moonlight Trail). From here the whole loop is pretty easy to follow with a few basic instructions.

The first 5 km are fun single track traversing the hillside above the Shotover River and then Moonlight Creek. The trail initially climbs gradually for 2 km with a few technical and rocky spots and amazing views. You can look down on the Fly By Wire adventure tourism site and back to the Shotover Jet, but you can also look onwards to the majestic countryside and a significant lack of tourists! Just as the trail starts to descend, ignore a track heading upwards to your left and continue up the valley.

The descent is a little tricky with strategically placed rocks, ruts and a little narrow track on a reasonably steep hillside. In places it could use trimming of the nasty, thorny matagouri bush, which is prolific around here. Bearing this in mind, make sure you have more spare tubes and puncture kits than normal. After this descent, the trail climbs again with a manageable gradient. There are a couple of cow-induced bogs to get around but the trail is otherwise mostly rideable with plenty of little challenges. The single track will come out on to a four-wheel drive road a little short of 5 km from the start, where you turn left up a steep rise. Shortly after this you will see a sign and track on your left towards Ben Lomond mountain, which you pass by — this will be at an obvious high point.

The four-wheel drive road is in good condition and after a little climb it drops right down to the Moke Creek. The climb out of the dip is nasty, but from here on it is cruisy right over to Moke Lake about 14 km from the start. As you near the lake you will pass behind an enormous shed and then go over a stile at a gate. Moke Lake has a beautiful DOC-administered camping area and is a popular spot for fishing, relaxing and low-key recreation. During summer sandfly-swatting features among the sports here also.

From here head right across the camping area and to the lake edge, where you will see a small bridge over a stream crossing. This is the start of the Moke

Lake circuit (anticlockwise), about 4 km of very pleasant lakeside single track. At the far end of the lake ignore the track to Lake Dispute and continue straight/left around the two arms of Moke Lake. At the end of the peninsula head hard right (not straight down the hill — it's a dead end), slightly up then down to an impressive boardwalk. The single track comes out on to the gravel road (the main Moke Lake Rd), where you head left and return to the gate at the camping ground. Should you wish, it is possible to turn right here and head up (yes, up), over the pass and down, ending up at the Seven Mile car park mentioned below (though it's road riding and thus highly not recommended).

From this point you head back the way you came along the four-wheel drive road, with a gentle climb, a steep down and a very steep up. Make sure you veer right at an intersection at about 26 km towards the Moonlight Track and on to the single track a kilometre or so after. The single-track return is great fun, with a rolling and challenging downhill that's not very steep, a couple of short climbs that probably need to be walked and a lovely couple of kilometres back to the car.

All in all, this is a great day out — it's a fun trail with magic terrain and Moke Lake is a perfect spot for a mid-ride swim and a picnic.

# **Seven Mile Point**

> 20+ kilometres
> 1–3 hours
> Skill level: all

Things have been changing at Seven Mile Point and the area is destined to become a significant mountain-biking destination in the Queenstown area. It is an area of tight XC-style single track that was being significantly added to in late 2007 to eventually give a total of 20–25 km of sweet trail riding.

At the time of writing a proposal for additional trails had been given the go-ahead and the funding and contractors were organised. The additional trails are to be purpose-built and professionally constructed and are due to open at the end of 2007.

**The riding**

To get to Seven Mile Point, head out of Queenstown towards Glenorchy for 7 km. Just past a road sign for Moke Lake on your right there is a gateway and large parking area on your left and some signage indicating this is Seven Mile. Parking here is a good plan.

From the main car park, you will follow the DOC dual-use track to the main area of mountain-bike trails. This track is clearly marked and heads out of the car park and steeply down a gravel path almost to the lake edge. A very pleasant piece of flowing single track carries you around the lake edge with a few technical rock sections and a wee stream to cross. There is a bit of pushing up some stairs as the trail heads away from the lake.

The lakeside headland of Seven Mile Point has great ground contour and is covered in native and exotic bush. There is plenty of scope for decent-length flowing trails and plenty of steep hillside for more technical stuff. Some good, fun mountain-bike trails have been here for a while and will be interconnected with all the new stuff being built.

After climbing away from the lake you will come to an entry point on your left, signposted for mountain-bike tracks. In here are Eldorado, Cloudburst and Bliss, which head back on to the main trail further along. Metolious and Loop 7 exit back in the direction you have come from, again on to the main trail. These are all great fun, flowing single track with some tight corners, obstacles and steep bits to keep you on your toes.

Further along the main dual-use trail another couple of mountain-bike trails are signed on the right. This is where Cool Runnings and IB55 start and by combining the two you can end up towards the end of the main track in the direction of Closeburn or Wilson Bay. Again, all these trails make the most of the natural terrain features, have been well constructed and are very cool. When the new tracks are finished there will be about three times more trails in this area. The proposal includes all levels of trail from beginner to advanced, but will continue to have a cross-country bias with an emphasis on great flow.

The Seven Mile tracks can be linked up with the easy Twelve Mile Delta to Bob's Cove single track. Head towards Glenorchy another four kilometres along the main road from Seven Mile then turn left at the Twelve Mile Delta Reserve sign. The track is about 6 km long and can be ridden in both directions.

# Fernhill Loop and Skyline

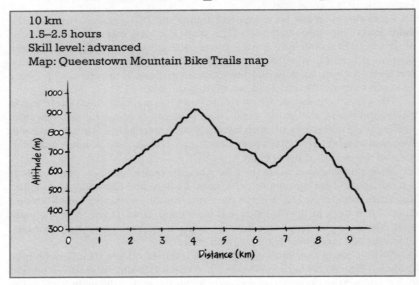

10 km
1.5–2.5 hours
Skill level: advanced
Map: Queenstown Mountain Bike Trails map

Skyline or Bob's Peak is the gondola hill in Queenstown. It is steep, pine covered and has some wild downhill riding. To the west a lovely single track known as the Fernhill Loop branches off and heads over to the suburb of Fernhill through rooty native forest.

The nicest way to ride the Fernhill Loop is not as a loop at all but as an up-and-back ride from the Skyline road, which maximises the super-fun single track. When you return from this track and are halfway up the Skyline road it would be rude not to ride to the top and head down the hill's signature mountain-bike trail Vertigo or one of its relatives.

**The riding**

The Skyline road is the gondola access road and is a well-formed dirt road that climbs relentlessly for about 400 vertical metres. The road is off Lomond Cres (which is accessed off Brunswick St from the lakefront). At the bottom of the hill there is a map board and the road is clearly signposted. Head on up and shortly you'll go around a gate. Before the gate is the exit trail (on your left heading up) — watch out for exiting riders, some may be control lacking. The gradient of the road is pretty mean, but the first bit is the worst. After 1.7 km you will come to an open area known as the midway clearing. Just past this on your left the Fernhill Loop track is signposted.

This is where the fun stuff begins. It is pretty much all uphill for nearly another 2 km but it is technical and challenging and the gradient is much easier going than the road climb. The track is initially quite smooth, then gets a bit rockier and rootier. After about 1.5 km you will come to a small stream crossing and after this things definitely get trickier. When it is entirely dry in here this would provide a great uphill challenge; when it is wet there is not much chance of making it up without some pushing. The track comes out of the trees into more open tussock land and the view from here is very cool. You are also more than 100 m higher than the gondola at this point and it can be a bit chilly up here. After a bit of a breather this is a great place to turn around. You can continue another kilometre or so to the grassy hilltop you can see ahead but this does require a down and uphill before you turn around and, although it is fun, it is a bit of a haul.

If you do want to ride over to Fernhill you just keep on going from here, but expect the downhill to be very steep switchbacks and not nearly as nice as what you have just come up. Having said that, this trail exits near to the legendary Dream and Mini Dream trails at the top of Fernhill. This is otherwise known as Wynyard Park and can be accessed off Wynyard Cres, Fernhill if you wish to drive up for a look or a ride later on.

The way back down is lovely, technical single-track fun, and in native forest as well; this is a real treat for skilled riders. It is just a pity it doesn't go on for longer! When you hit the Skyline road again, pause to appreciate what you have just experienced and then head left and continue on up the road.

About 1.2 km further up the hill and just below the gondola building you can see a well-marked mountain-bike trail, Vertigo, on your right. It is a downhill-only track suitable for intermediate-plus level riders and has a number of side tracks and variations off it. The terrain is a bit rocky, a bit rooty and reasonably steep. There are jumps if you want them and some berms to encourage the flow as you speed on down this cool track.

The track crosses the main Skyline road a number of times and you need to be prepared to slow down for these crossings to avoid pedestrians (generally tourists too tight to pay for the gondola), cars (rare) and bikers (please don't hit them) going both up and down the road. The trail is generally well signposted and it is easy enough to follow your nose down the hill. Be on the lookout for some of the side options, which are marked, and bear in mind that most of these are more technical than the main trail. Back at the midway clearing on the far side of the open area the sign now says 'Mountain bike trail' and is the easiest and clearest way back down to the bottom of the Skyline road.

# Skippers Pack Track

8 km loop
1 hour
Skill level: intermediate

The Skippers Pack Track is an old gold-mining track into Skippers Canyon. It is a one-way downhill blast in amazing countryside. The ride back to the start on the infamous Skippers Rd is surprisingly pleasant for an uphill on the road. In addition there is a very fine single track known as the Zoot Track back on to the Coronet Peak road.

 ## The riding

The Skippers Pack Track starts from the Skippers Saddle just off the Coronet Peak road. To get here from Queenstown head out of town on Gorge Rd, through Arthur's Point and turn left after 12 km on the Coronet Peak ski field road. About 4 km up this road turn left onto Skippers Rd and less than 1 km along here you will see the obvious saddle and parking area. On the left is the Mt Dewar car park — this is a rideable half-day loop of mostly paddock racing but does have some spectacular scenery. On your right (gate and cattle-stop ahead) is your car park.

Get on your bike at the saddle and cross the cattle-stop on the main road. You will be able to see the pack track in the gully to the right of the road — and it will look like fun! Head off down the track, not forgetting to pause and look at the amazing terrain.

The trail is almost all downhill, and is fun, fast and flowing as well as being perfect biking width. Not much more needs to be said! After 3.5 km the trail fords a small stream, climbs, and heads down again. Crossing the stream at the bottom of the hill (on a small bridge) has you on the Skippers Rd about 5 km from the saddle. From here you pretty much have to head left and ride back up the road to the top of the trail. This trail will continue to be fun even if you are forced to ride it more than once, which is a popular option, especially as it's a perfect shuttle-accessible ride. The trail is not very technically challenging but with a little more pace on there is plenty to think about.

A little treat that can be added to the trip up the Coronet Peak road is to head down from the saddle back towards Queenstown via the Zoot Track. It is only about 1 km long and there is no sign for it but you will know it when you are on the track. On the Queenstown side of the saddle there is a flat area and on the far side of this you will be able to see a trail traversing the hillside. This is it; you can't get lost. It has a few more jumps and bumps than the Skippers Track and is nice piece of trail. You may like to follow or scout the landings first (the jumps are not compulsory). It meets the Coronet Peak road not very far down the hill and you can ride back up or arrange someone to drive down.

You could also combine these little rides with a look at the Coronet Peak trails in summer. At the Coronet Peak ski field there is a purpose-built and marked XC and downhill course. Both can be accessed off the lifts during the short open season in summer. For details see www.nzski.com.

 **Coffee and food**

Queenstown has more options for coffee, food and drinks than you could ever need. If you are perplexed by the selection or just need to get to a good coffee quickly try Joe's Garage (15 Camp St) or Vudu (23 Beach St). There is also a

Joe's Garage in Arrowtown (7 Arrow Lane) which is excellent and they both have great breakfasts.

There are way too many restaurants for dinner to even make a call on where to go but The Cow (Cow Lane) is tucked out of sight of most of the tourists and has great pizza and loads of atmosphere.

## Accommodation

Queenstown has a truckload of upmarket accommodation options and a lot of backpackers. If you are flying in there may be a good package deal including accommodation otherwise you will have to wade through some options.

If you like a little more wilderness, the DOC campsite at Moke Lake is beautiful. You could ride the Moonlight Track and around the lake from here and you could also ride down to Seven Mile or Twelve Mile Delta via the Lake Dispute Track. If you want to stay out of the hustle of a very busy tourist town this could be the spot for you. There is also a DOC campsite at Twelve Mile Delta.

## Things to do

If you want other outdoor recreation that won't cost you a fortune, there is a lot of stunning walking to be done around Queenstown. The Wakatipu Trails walking map is readily available from DOC and visitor information. A wander up Ben Lomond will give you a great view and perspective on the town but it is a big walk for pedallers' legs. The Mt Crichton Loop trail (otherwise known as Sam Summers) near Twelve Mile Delta is a nice walk but would make a better mountain-bike ride if you were allowed.

You can also run, walk, ride or four-wheel drive your way up to the classic destination of Macetown. A few river crossings will bring rewards. It starts from Arrowtown — head up the Arrow River and go left. Not to be attempted in the rain.

If you are keen for a swim in Lake Wakatipu then the town lakefront, Sunshine Bay, Frankton Arm or the Seven Mile and Twelve Mile areas are options. Moke Lake is a nice spot too.

Again, like everything around Queenstown, there are plenty of activities and a hundred expensive adrenalin thrills to be had. The choice is yours and there is certainly plenty of information available.

A wander through historic Arrowtown is a worthy excursion from the masses, although the popularity of this picturesque wee place is not to be underestimated.

In the Gibbston Valley some stunning wineries occupy the terraces above the Kawarau River and will be tempting if you have interests in this area.

A little more out of the way but an amazing drive is a visit to Glenorchy. The scenery itself makes the trip worthy and the Glenorchy Café is pretty good too.

 **Other rides**

The Arawata Bridle Track and Sunshine Bay Track are always worth a look. Head out of Queenstown towards Seven Mile, go straight at the roundabout, along a bit and hang a right up the far side of Fernhill Rd (at Sunshine Bay). Take the first left, roll around up to Arawata Tce and on your left is the Arawata Bridle trail. About 10 to 15 minutes along it, you will end up on the road, go left, along a bit, then right down to the Sunshine Bay boat ramp. The Sunshine Bay trail is on the left. Both are nice, but short.

There's also a trail to Frankton. It's a lakefront ride, a bit disrupted but worth a look if you would like to have a nosey up the arm. The track starts from the waterfront in Queenstown. You can join this up with the Kelvin Heights and Jacks Point Walkway if you wish. Neither of these involves technical biking but are just nice rolling trails.

There's a pump/jump park at the Arrowtown end of Gorge Rd.

---

### Contacts
**Bike shops**: Outside Sports (Shotover St), Bike Fix (Gorge Rd), Vertigo (Brecon St)
**Queenstown visitor information centre**: corner Shotover and Camp streets, 03 442 4100, www.queenstown-vacation.com

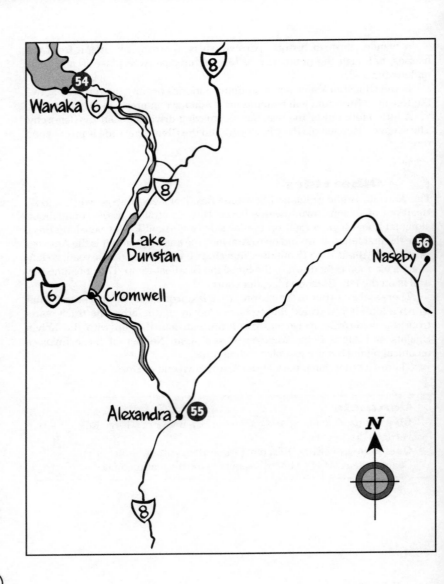

# Central Otago

**Central Otago has hot and dry summers, wicked landscapes and some fantastic mountain biking. You could happily spend a weekend in any of the three locations chosen for this chapter, cruising around some lovely trails and relaxing in the salubrious atmosphere. This package picks out some of the best trail riding and takes a driving tiki tour through some awesome countryside. It would be ideal to spread this selection out over a week or an Easter break but it could also be an action-filled and busy long weekend. If you have plenty of time there is also no shortage of other riding around these parts, especially of the open-countryside epic variety.**

Wanaka is great fun and you can't help loving the trails. There is opportunity for everyone on the purpose-built tree-covered trails and plenty to develop your skills on. Alexandra is wild, open-country riding on parched trails with fragrant air. There's plenty of riding for all skill levels and you can make things as tough as you like both up and downhill depending on your speed.

The access issues in Alexandra mean that you'll need to tap into some local knowledge to find the real gold of the riding here. And then there is Naseby, a cute town with trail-riding fun for everyone.

# Sticky Forest, Wanaka

> 2–4 hours
> Skill level: all
> Map: Lake Wanaka Cycling Map

Sticky Forest, also known as the Plantation Trails, is a very cool mountain-biking spot. It is a tight collection of hand-built mountain-bike specific trails providing hours of entertainment. With flowing downhills (and uphills), beautifully bermed corners, a whole family of gap jumps and some forest so dense you almost need a torch, this is a fun place to pedal away some time.

If you have not ridden here before you should definitely get a map. These are available from a number of places including bike and outdoor shops and the information centre. The map is colour coded for difficulty and numbered and shows a couple of other tracks in the area, including the very scenic Outlet Track.

## The riding

To find Sticky Forest head out of the main part of Wanaka north around the lake edge on Lakeside Rd, veer right on to Beacon Point Rd, then right into Aubrey Rd and left into Rata St. In 2007 Rata St finished at a dead end where subdivision earthworks were in progress. From this point you head right, up towards the forest on a dirt track until you reach the named riding tracks. It seems likely that this access point will be altered in some way as the urban sprawl encroaches.

The pine plantation has a very fine rock/sand hard-packed aggregate base. Many of the trails have been around for a long time and are well ridden and worn, forming a dusty, almost concrete-like, surface. In summer the dense forest shades these trails, which is good, and on wet days it provides some shelter. They are effectively year-round trails as this area gets minimal lasting snow in the winter and is readily rideable after it rains.

The first track from the Rata St entrance is Hoe Down, and a very nice way to head up into the forest it is. At the top of Hoe Down you will meet Easy Street and by heading right along here will take yourself into the thick of a squiggly web of trail goodness.

With the map indicating which tracks are up, down or both, and the good signposting you really can just taste whichever trails take your fancy. From this side all the trails off to the right of the wide Easy Street convene at the downhill end at what is known as The Hub. From there you can take your pick of a number of uphill trails back to the top and try something else or do it all again. You can ride the ones you like best again and again or you can try to ride them all.

Venus (#8) is one that definitely shouldn't be missed, and its uphill return trail Crankin Fine (#26) is famous for its spiral with an overpass bridge, a fine piece of engineering. Yumpts (#13) has gap jumps on it of increasing size that make perfect practice terrain for gradually increasing your jumping confidence. Somewhere in there is an amazing see-saw and, even if you have no intention of riding it, you should see it!

Sticky Forest is one of those places that you appreciate on your first visit but riding there again when you know where to head and what to expect allows you to practise getting faster and smoother on twisting tight trails. It's also a great deal of fun.

The mighty Clutha River exits Lake Wanaka just below the Sticky Forest; this provides some spectacularly clear blue water, outstanding views and a lovely roll-along trail along its bank, potentially ending in Albert Town. The track is a popular walking trail so be wary of your speed. To get there, either ride from the end of Beacon Point Rd or drop down from the Sticky Forest. From the forest, beware that all the trails have steep parts, unless you ride the 'road' down from The Hub.

As you descend you will notice a number of trails coming out of the dry creeks on your right — these are mostly steep and nice (but short) downhill trails. The tracks here tend to be older than the forest trails and not so well marked; do not be surprised if you find yourself in an unexpected place — but don't worry, find the river again and you can't go wrong.

# 55

# Alexandra

50–70 km
1 hour to a whole day
Skill level: all

Alexandra is another semi-legendary Central Otago port of call for mountain bikers. The landscape is treeless, dry and hard-packed and the wild thyme covering the hillsides famously fragrances the air. The riding here is unique, with well-formed trails rolling with the lie of the land in wild, hilly countryside with a desert feel. The sun burns hot in the summer and with no shade you need to be careful. In winter it is usually still very rideable as long as you can keep your feet warm.

Most people from out of town who love riding in Alexandra will tell you that you need to know a local to really have fun here. The difficulty with the very fine single track in the area behind the 'clock on the hill' is that it is on private land, and a working farm at that. Although the land is covered in sensational trails they are not advertised or well marked and getting clear information can be tricky.

It is pretty well accepted that the original marked trail, which is two loops with yellow and red metal markers, is freely accessible for mountain bikers and the landowner seems to be happy with this. It is, however, still private land and being able to use these trails is a privilege and is thanks to considerable goodwill from the farmer (and the understanding that some of the area has restricted access during the lambing season).

 **The riding**

The red and yellow marked loops are about 15 km each when done separately or about 22 km when done together, as they share the same climb. To find these trails head out of the main part of Alexandra and cross the Shaky Bridge, a narrow pedestrian bridge signposted off Tarbert St (the road to Ranfurly). You will be heading towards the famous clock on the hill. Turn left over the bridge, eye up the nice-looking café there for later and follow a trail near the road until you cross over Little Valley Rd and head on to Tucker Hill Rd. This road has a bunch of fun single tracks beside it. Head along here and cross the Central Otago Rail Trail twice, keeping a keen eye out for a four-wheel drive track heading off to the right, which is marked with the yellow and red metal markers. From here the marked tracks are well worn and have been around for a while. You essentially head up the hill and then peel off to the right on the red track to loop around and return to the main uphill track, or head a little further up the hill and follow the markers around to the left to loop back down and eventually join up to the rail trail. This is all pretty easy to follow and good fun but certainly not the tastiest of what is on offer in Alexandra.

Another way to get some perspective on a few local trails is to take a scenic drive (or ride) up to the lookout marked on Little Valley Rd. Cast your eye away from town and you will begin to see the type of trails that you could be riding a little further afield with the right local knowledge.

So . . . to find the real riding in Alexandra you need to head to the local bike shop and mountain-bike guiding business. Phil from Altitude Adventures is the knowledgeable local you need to know to have a fantastic time here. He can provide you with a bit of a map of the local trails and point you in the right direction for the duration and type of riding you want.

Probably one of the best options to get the most out of this place is to head out on a trip with one of the Altitude Adventures guides. They know their way around the Alex trails and they have an arrangement with the local landowner that reduces any tension and discomfort about riding around here.

Altitude Adventures/Henderson Cycles in Centennial Ave is open during the week and Saturday mornings. Ring in advance for organising guided trips or if you need some assistance.

**56**

# Naseby Forest

| |
|---|
| 25–30 km |
| 1–2 days |
| Skill level: all |
| Map: Naseby Forest Recreation Area map |

Naseby Forest is somewhat legendary as a Central Otago mountain-biking destination. It is a riding oasis of trees, water and narrow flowing single track in countryside bereft of much of this style of riding, and where the typical landscape lends itself to open and exposed farm-type tracks.

The historic gold-mining town of Naseby is 12 km north of Ranfurly. The turn-off is marked off State Highway 85. The main town is based around Derwent St and consists of several hotels and cafés, the information and craft centre, Kila's Bike Shop and an array of historic buildings. With most of the Naseby area above 600 m elevation the climate is hot in the summer and cold in the winter.

Despite some claims that the free-draining soil means it is all-weather riding terrain, the best advice is not to ride here in the rain. The forest is clay-based — this is slippery and sticky when wet, usually outweighing the enjoyment factor! However, all is not lost because it does dry very fast indeed and a few more coffees may see you right while the surface improves.

The Naseby Forest recreation area is north-west of the small town and is accessible from several points. The forest is a privately owned working pine plantation with a significant area accessible for recreation (mostly mountain biking and walking). The area is criss-crossed with excellent and fun single-track, historic gold trails and four-wheel drive tracks.

 **The riding**

It is definitely helpful to have a map of the recreation area and you can get these from Kila's Bike Shop or the Royal Hotel in town. The map shows the main roads, four-wheel drive roads and trails in the forest but doesn't show all of the ever-improving mountain-bike trails.

One way to get orientated in the forest is to ride the section of the Mt Ida water-race that passes through here. This is a wide, flat trail suitable for all riders and, although not technically fun or challenging, will help you get your bearings. To find it, head straight up Hog Burn Gully, turning left when you meet it. By following it all the way to the west side of the forest you will come out near the Coal Pit Dam.

From the Coal Pit Dam to Translator Rd the trails are suitable for all levels of mountain bikers. This area is bisected by Hoffmans Dam Rd and Wet Gully Rd running north to south so if you feel lost or are looking for your next trail you'll find that most of the trails cross these roads. To the east side of Translator

Rd, the trails are significantly more technical and better suited to intermediate and advanced riders.

North of the lookout the trails take another step up and are best suited to more advanced riders. The terrain in this area is wild and Utah-esque with eroded spines, canyons and weather-sculpted cliffs. This area is filled with technical stuff and many jumps and drops plus rooty technical challenges for contenders.

Closer to the camping ground, and heading off to the left from Hog Burn Gully, the trails are in the more dense pine plantation with short rideable uphills and flowing, tight single-track downhills. You will constantly be spying little trails all around these parts worthy of checking out so you may end up riding bits and pieces numerous times to cover all the good parts. Several small bridges across the water-race lead on to tracks.

It is always difficult to make sure that you cover the best trails an area has to offer when you ride there for the first time. The Royal Hotel and bike shop staff are really helpful at pointing you toward specific trails if you need some help. Planning a couple of days here will ensure you find most of the trail riding in the forest and get to ride your favourite stuff a few times.

 **Coffee and food**

Wanaka has a good selection of cafés and other fine food and drink places. The Ardmore St Food Company (under the Speight's bar) at 155 Ardmore St comes highly recommended for its café, deli and bakery. Café Gusto, 1 Lakeside Rd, has great coffee and is on the way to Sticky Forest.

In Alexandra you may like to try the well-positioned Shaky Bridge Vineyard Café. It is right opposite the Shaky Bridge and under the clock on the hill on the other side of the Manuherikia River. Right in town, try Side Walk Café (72 Centennial Ave) and the Blues Lounge (49 Centennial Ave).

Despite its size Naseby has several cafés and a couple of pubs too. The Royal Hotel on the main street has good coffee, snacks and pub-style meals and the nearby Black Forest Café also does good coffee and home cooking. If you plan to head a little further afield the Danseys Pass Coach Inn restaurant has a good reputation.

# Accommodation

Wanaka has a huge collection of hotels and motels and numerous backpackers. There are loads of upmarket options but if you are looking to stay somewhere a little more low-key or to camp you could try the quiet and scenic Outlet Motor Camp (Lake Outlet Rd), which links up to Sticky Forest by single track. Glendhu Bay Motor Camp (11 km from Wanaka on Mt Aspiring Rd) is scenic and on the lake shores but very busy in holiday times. The Albert Town Reserve DOC campsite (5 km north-east of Wanaka on State Highway 6) is worth a look, especially in the off season.

Alexandra has motels and backpackers and a couple of holiday parks for camping. If you are looking for something a bit out of the way between Naseby and Alexandra check out the Poolburn Dam. It is a bit of a drive off the main road but is in fantastic countryside and you could easily pitch a tent.

The Naseby Larchview Holiday Park is classic mountain-biker accommodation and they have cabins as well as campsites. The Royal Hotel has nice-looking accommodation with double, twin and bunk rooms. If you are heading over from Danseys Pass, the Coach Inn is pretty sweet looking but much more upmarket.

# Things to do

In Wanaka you can dip in for a swim at the main waterfront, Eely Point, or hunt around for some swimming holes in the Clutha or Hawea rivers when it is hot. Paddle or tube down the Clutha or take a jet ski for a skid.

If you are looking for some pedestrian activity, the walk up Mt Iron (about an hour to the top) is popular for its stunning views. For more exertion, the track up Mt Roy (five to six hours return) is a good workout and there are also plenty of options around the Matukituki Valley in Mt Aspiring National Park, including the Rob Roy Glacier and Aspiring Hut. If it is raining on the real rock, try the indoor climbing at Basecamp Wanaka.

Wanaka has a multitude of tourist activities and plenty of information on these. The Paradiso movie theatre is a local institution.

Naseby is home to the Southern Hemisphere's only dedicated curling rink. It is a plush new facility in Channel Rd, open year-round, with tuition and hireage at very reasonable prices. In the winter there is an outdoor skating rink next to it.

Naseby has numerous historic buildings from the gold-mining era and you can wander around the town with the guidance of a historic walking-tour pamphlet.

It's worth considering a drive over Danseys Pass. It is a beautiful trip through old mining country and passes through the Kyeburn Diggings area, which has evidence of old mining operations.

 ## Other rides

Other rides worth looking into if you have more time include the Millennium Track and the Lakeside Track in Wanaka, a gentle roll-around that gets so busy in summer it almost needs traffic lights; the Old Man Range — if riding grass fast is your thing look closely at this option; and Wanaka Station to Minaret Burn. This is mostly a four-wheel drive track, with a short walking-track section and a big hill climb, fantastic scenery and beaches.

There is also the option of chairlift riding at Cardrona/Treble Cone during the season, and of course the Central Otago Rail Trail — New Zealand's premier mountain-bike tour, taking in marvellous Central Otago countryside on a flat-tish gravel track.

## Contacts

**Lake Wanaka visitor information centre**: 100 Ardmore St, Wanaka, 03 443 1233, www.lakewanaka.co.nz
**Central Otago visitor information centre**: 21 Centennial Ave, Alexandra, 03 448 9515
**Altitude Adventures/Henderson Cycles:** 88 Centennial Ave, Alexandra, 03 448 8917, 021 456 918, www.altitudeadventures.co.nz
**Kila's Bike Shop**: 20 Derwent St, Naseby, 03 444 9088, email kilasbikeshop@gmail.com

# Index